**Cultural and
Geographical
Exploration**

Grand Canyon Experiences

CHRONICLES FROM *NATIONAL GEOGRAPHIC*

Cultural and Geographical Exploration

**Cultural and
Geographical
Exploration**

Grand Canyon Experiences

CHRONICLES FROM *NATIONAL GEOGRAPHIC*

Arthur M. Schlesinger, jr.
Senior Consulting Editor

Fred L. Israel
General Editor

CHELSEA HOUSE PUBLISHERS

Philadelphia

CHELSEA HOUSE PUBLISHERS

Editor in Chief Stephen Reginald
Managing Editor James D. Gallagher
Production Manager Pamela Loos
Art Director Sara Davis
Director of Photography Judy L. Hasday
Senior Production Editor LeeAnne Gelletly

© 2000 by Chelsea House Publishers, a division of
Main Line Book Co. All rights reserved. Printed and bound in the United States of America.

The Chelsea House World Wide Web site address is
http://www.chelseahouse.com

First Printing

1 3 5 7 9 8 6 4 2

Library of Congress Cataloging-in-Publication Data

Library of Congress Cataloging-in-Publication Data

Experiences in the Grand Canyon / National Geographic Society.
        p.   cm. - (Cultural & geographical exploration: chronicles
from National Geographic)
        Based on articles originally appearing in National geographic.
        Includes index.
        Summary: Text originally published in "National Geographic" describes
travels through the Grand Canyon in the early years of the twentieth
century, when it was relatively unexplored.
        ISBN 0-7910-5442-X
    1.   Grand Canyon (Ariz.) - Description and travel Juvenile literature.
    2.   Grand Canyon (Ariz.) - Discovery and exploration Juvenile literature.
    3.   Grand Canyon (Ariz.) Pictorial works Juvenile literature.
    [1. Grand Canyon (Ariz.)] I. National Geographic Society (U.S.)
II. National geographic.   III. Series: Cultural and geographical exploration.
F788.E97   1999
917.91'320453-dc21   99-24929
                                   CIP

CONTENTS

"THE GREATEST EDUCATIONAL JOURNAL"

When the first *National Geographic* magazine appeared in October 1888, the United States totaled 38 states. Grover Cleveland was President. The nation's population hovered around 60 million. Great Britain's Queen Victoria also ruled as the Empress of India. William II became Kaiser of Germany that year. Czar Alexander III ruled Russia, and the Turkish Empire stretched from the Balkans to the tip of Arabia. To Westerners, the Far East was still a remote and mysterious land. Throughout the world, riding the back of an animal was the principal means of transportation. Unexplored and unmarked places dotted the global map.

On January 13, 1888, thirty-three men—scientists, cartographers, inventors, scholars, and explorers—met in Washington, D.C. They had accepted an invitation from Gardiner Greene Hubbard (1822–1897), the first president of the Bell Telephone Company and a leader in the education of the deaf, to form the National Geographic Society "to increase and diffuse geographic knowledge." One of the assembled group noted that they were the "first explorers of the Grand Canyon and the Yellowstone, those who had carried the American flag farthest north, who had measured the altitude of our famous mountains, traced the windings of our coasts and rivers, determined the distribution of flora and fauna, enlightened us in the customs of the aborigines, and marked out the path of storm and flood." Nine months later, the first issue of *National Geographic* magazine was sent out to 165 charter members. Today, more than a century later, membership has grown to an astounding 11 million in more than 170 nations. Several times that number regularly read the monthly issues of the *National Geographic* magazine.

The first years were difficult ones for the new magazine. The earliest volumes seem dreadfully scientific and quite dull. The articles in Volume I, No. 1 set the tone—W. M. Davis, "Geographic Methods in Geologic Investigation," followed by W. J. McGee, "The Classification of Geographic Forms by Genesis." Issues came out erratically—three in 1889, five in 1890, four in 1891; and two in 1895. In January 1896 "an illustrated monthly" was added to the title. The November issue that year contained a photograph of a half-naked Zulu bride and bridegroom in their wedding finery staring full face into the camera. But, a reader must have wondered what to make of the accompanying text: "These people . . . possess some excellent traits, but are horribly cruel when once they have smelled blood." In hopes of expanding circulation, the Board of Managers offered newsstand copies at $.25 each and began to accept advertising. But the magazine essentially remained unchanged. Circulation rose only slightly.

In January 1898, shortly after Gardiner Greene Hubbard's death, his son-in-law Alexander Graham Bell (1847–1922) agreed to succeed him as the second president of the National Geographic Society. Bell invented the telephone in 1876 and, while pursuing his lifelong goal of improving the lot of the deaf, had turned his amazingly versatile mind to contemplating such varied problems as human flight, air conditioning, and popularizing geography. The society then had about 1,100 members—the magazine was on the edge of bankruptcy. Bell did not want the job. He wrote in his diary, though, that he accepted leadership of the society "in order to save it." "Geography is a fascinating subject and it can be made interesting," he told the board of directors. Bell abandoned the unsuccessful attempt to increase circulation through newsstand sales. "Our journal," he wrote, "should go to members, people who believe in our work and want to help." He understood that the lure for prospective members should be an association with a society that made it possible for the average person to share with kings and scientists the excitement of sending an expedition to a strange land or an explorer to an inaccessible region. This idea, more than any other, has been responsible for the growth of the National Geographic Society and for the popularity of the magazine. "I can well remember," recalled Bell in 1912, "how the idea was laughed at that we should ever reach a membership of ten thousand." That year it had soared to 107,000!

Bell attributed this phenomenal growth, though, to one man who had transformed the *National Geographic* magazine into "the greatest educational journal in the world"—Gilbert H. Grosvenor (1875–1966). Bell had hired Grosvenor, then 24, in 1899 as the National Geographic Society's first full-time employee, "to put some life into the magazine." He personally escorted the new editor, who would become his son-in-law, to the society's headquarters—a small rented room shared with the American Forestry Association on the fifth floor of a building near the U.S. Treasury in downtown Washington. Grosvenor remembered the headquarters "littered with old magazines, newspapers, and a few record books and six enormous boxes crammed with *Geographics* returned by the newsstands." "No desk!" exclaimed Bell. "I'll send you mine." That afternoon, delivery men brought Grosvenor a large walnut rolltop and the new editor began to implement Bell's instructions—to transform the magazine from one of cold geographic fact "expressed in hieroglyphic terms which the layman could not understand into a vehicle for carrying the living, breathing, human-interest truth about this great world of ours to the people." And what did Bell consider appropriate "geographic subjects"? He replied: "The world and all that is in it is our theme."

Grosvenor shared Bell's vision of a great society and magazine that would disseminate geographic knowledge. "I thought of geography in terms of its Greek root: *geographia*—a description of the world," he later wrote. "It thus becomes the most catholic of subjects, universal in appeal, and embracing nations, people, plants, birds, fish. We would never lack interesting subjects." To attract readers, Grosvenor had to change the public attitude toward geography, which he knew was regarded as "one of the dullest of all subjects, something to inflict upon schoolboys and avoid in later life." He wondered why certain books that relied heavily on geographic description remained popular—Charles Darwin's *Voyage of the Beagle*, Richard Dana Jr.'s *Two Years Before the Mast*, and even Herodotus's *History*. Why did readers for generations—and with Herodotus's travels, for 20 centuries—return to these books? What did these volumes, which used so many geographic descriptions, have in common? What was the secret? According to Grosvenor, the answer was that "each was an accurate, eyewitness, firsthand account. Each contained simple straightforward writing—writing that sought to make pictures in the reader's mind."

Gilbert Grosvenor was editor of the *National Geographic* magazine for 55 years, from 1899 until 1954. Each of the 660 issues under his direction had been a highly readable geography textbook. He took Bell's vision and made it a reality. Acclaimed as "Mr. Geography," he discovered the earth anew for himself and for millions around the globe. He charted the dynamic course that the National Geographic Society and its magazine followed for more than half a century. In so doing, he forged an instrument for world education and understanding unique in this or any age. Under his direction, the *National Geographic* magazine grew in circulation from a few hundred copies—he recalled carrying them to the post office on his back—to more than five million at the time of his retirement as editor, enough for a stack 25 miles high.

This Chelsea House series celebrates Grosvenor's first 25 years as editor of the *National Geographic*. "The mind must see before it can believe," said Grosvenor. From the earliest days, he filled the magazine with photographs and established another Geographic principle—to portray people in their natural attire or lack of it. Within his own editorial committee, young Grosvenor encountered the prejudice that photographs had to be "scientific." Too often, this meant dullness. To Grosvenor, every picture and sentence had to be interesting to the layperson. "How could you educate and inform if you lost your audience by boring your readers?" Grosvenor would ask his staff. He persisted and succeeded in making the *National Geographic* magazine reflect this fascinating world.

To the young-in-heart of every age there is magic in the name *National Geographic*. The very words conjure up enchanting images of faraway places, explorers and scientists, sparkling seas and dazzling mountain peaks, strange plants, animals, people, and customs. The small society founded in 1888 "for the increase and diffusion of geographic knowledge" grew, under the guidance of one man, to become a great force for knowledge and understanding. This achievement lies in the genius of Gilbert H. Grosvenor, the architect and master builder of the National Geographic Society and its magazine.

Fred L. Israel
The City College of the City University of New York

GRAND CANYON EXPERIENCES

FRED L. ISRAEL

The Grand Canyon is one of the most spectacular natural formations in the world. Statistics can hardly suggest its vastness. Although photographs have been taken from hundreds of different points of view, no image can truly capture its beauty. The canyon cuts across northwestern Arizona for more than 215 miles, the width ranging from less than one-half mile to almost 18 miles, and the height reaching a vertical drop of about one mile. For some six million years, the Colorado River has flowed through the canyon, sculpting and cutting through layers of limestone, sandstone, and other rocks. At an average speed of four miles per hour, the river flows west, then turns south to eventually empty into the Gulf of California in Mexico. More than 300 species of birds and 120 kinds of animals abound in the area. Adding to the Grand Canyon's mystical allure is the fact that it is constantly changing, as its walls reshape themselves due to weather and river erosion. Surrounding the Grand Canyon is the 1,000-square mile Grand Canyon National Park, which the United States established in 1919. Today, it is one of the nation's most popular parks, visited by over four million people a year.

The first known Europeans to view the canyon in 1540 were not impressed. They found neither a marvel nor a spectacle, but an unconquerable obstacle hindering their advance. These Spanish explorers, led by Garcia Lopez de Cardenas, had been sent to this area by Francisco Coronado in his continuing search for signs of the legendary Seven Golden Cities of Cibola—which, of course, did not exist. Cardenas spent three days looking for a way to descend to the Colorado River before retracing his path to the Hopi village from which his troops had come. Having nothing analogous against which to make comparisons, Cardenas reported that some of the boulders in the canyon were "bigger than the great tower of Seville."

American trappers and explorers penetrated the canyon region during the first half of the 19th century. Finally, in 1857, the United States War Department sent Lt. Joseph Ives, a recent West Point graduate, to explore the Colorado River. From an iron steamer that had been built in Philadelphia and shipped in sections via Panama and San Francisco, Ives made a minute hydrographic survey. Forced to abandon the unwieldy ship where the Colorado River enters the canyon, Ives and his party continued the journey in rowboats and then on foot. His 1861 "Report Upon the Colorado River of the West" and reports of the scientists accompanying his expedition made a major contribution to understanding this little known and superficially explored region. The vivid descriptions in Ives's report received accolades from his superiors. However, one of the conclusions must rank Ives among history's worst prophets: "The region last explored is, of course, altogether valueless. It can be approached only from the south, and after entering there is nothing to do but to leave. Ours has been the first, and will doubtless be the last, party of whites to visit this profitless locality. It seems intended by nature that the Colorado river, along the greater portion of its lonely and majestic way, shall be forever unvisited and undisturbed."

John Wesley Powell has the distinction of being the first white person to traverse the Grand Canyon by boat, following the Colorado River. Powell, a geologist, would organize and lead groups of students and amateur naturalists across the Great Plains to the Rocky Mountains. It was while on one of these trips that Powell first saw the gorges of the Colorado River and conceived of the daring scheme of exploring them using boats. On May 24, 1869, financed by the Smithsonian Institute and an appropriation from Congress, his party of nine men and four boats began their journey. They emerged safely from the mouth of the Grand Canyon on August 29th, having travelled nearly 900 miles. Powell made two other voyages through the canyon in 1871–72. The results of his explorations were published in 1875.

In 1903, President Theodore Roosevelt visited the Grand Canyon. His vision was no longer of conquering the wilderness, but of preserving it. Roosevelt stated:

> Grand Canyon Arizona was a natural wonder which, so far as I know, is in kind absolutely unparalleled throughout the rest of the world . . . Leave it as it is. You cannot improve upon it. The ages have been at work on it, and man can only mar it. What you can do is to keep it for your children, your children's children, and for all those who come after you as one of the great sights which every American can, if he can travel at all, should see.

Sixteen years later, the most spectacular portions of the Colorado River and much of the surrounding area became a national park, forever protected from commercial exploitation.

Since 1893, *National Geographic* has published more than 25 articles about the Grand Canyon. The Kolb article included in this compilation is seminal, being the first photographic essay to appear about the Grand Canyon in a major periodical. The brothers Ellsworth and Emery Kolb spent 12 years exploring practically every part of the canyon. At one point, they duplicated John Wesley Powell's famous 1869 river journey, carrying their heavy camera equipment along with them. Their outstanding photographs, which first appeared in *National Geographic*, are some of the earliest photographic records of the unequaled scenic wonders of the southwest. These marvelous pictures give a graphic conception of the dangers encountered in compiling such an account, as well as a glimpse of the extraordinary characters of Ellsworth and Emery Kolb, two of America's prominent explorers.

Also included in this book is a sprightly description of the newly constructed suspension bridge over the Colorado River, written by Harriet Chalmers Adams. Between 1907 and 1937, Mrs. Adams published 21 articles in the *National Geographic*, ranking her among the most prolific contributors to the magazine.

VOL. XXVI, No. 2   WASHINGTON   AUGUST, 1914

EXPERIENCES IN
THE GRAND CANYON

BY ELLSWORTH AND EMERY KOLB

For twelve years the authors of this article, Messrs. Ellsworth and Emery Kolb have lived at the head of the Bright Angel trail, in the Grand Canyon of Arizona. From this headquarters they have penetrated to practically all parts of the Grand Canyon and of its less-known tributary canyons. Always they have taken their cameras with them, for their primary object has been to obtain a complete photographic record of the unequaled scenic wonders of the Southwest for the enjoyment and instruction of the millions of Americans who are unable to visit them. The first part of this article describes a trip to what is considered the most beautiful of the tributary canyons, the Cataract Creek Canyon; the second part a hard journey to the canyon of the Little Colorado, and the third part their "big trip" as Messrs. Kolb call it, a duplication of Major Powell's famous journey down the Green and Colorado rivers. To accomplish this feat they passed through seventeen canyons, with a total descent on the river of 6,000 feet. The marvelous photographs published with this article give a graphic conception of the dangers encountered and of the extraordinary character and grandeur of this most stupendous chasm.

I
A JOURNEY TO
CATARACT CREEK CANYON

OURS was no triumphal entry as we toiled our weary way through the little village of Havasupai Indians, in the bottom of Havasu, or Cataract Canyon, 50 miles west of the Bright Angel trail, in the Grand Canyon, one of us astride a mule as weary as ourselves, the other walking, while one of our two pack-burros, with his precious load of cameras and dry plates, stampeded down the road, trying to shake off some yelping curs that were following at his heels. The other burro, meanwhile, was standing his ground and was circling after his particular opponents, striking at them with his fore feet with all the celerity of a boxer.

Many of the 200 natives were amusedly watching the performance. They especially enjoyed our own efforts to appear unconcerned

"CAPTAIN BURRO"

Gazing at "The Bridal Veil Falls" in Havasu Canyon, Cataract Creek, probably the most beautiful of all the lateral canyons which empty into the Colorado River. It was a chilly September morn, and the mist rising from the falls gave him an uncomfortable bath.

and yet keep our eye on the pack of vicious dogs that had rushed upon us so suddenly. Some young bucks, frequent visitors to the Grand Canyon, grinned and nudged each other when we were almost dismounted by a sudden spasm on the part of the mule, as a dog finally laid hold of his heel. The dog flattened himself out on his belly as the mule's feet twinkled harmlessly over his head.

Then "Captain Burro" came out with a club and stones and drove the dogs to the bushes. The Captain was an old acquaintance, as were many of the other Indians, and this time at least we were glad to see him. Extending his hand in greeting, with his thin-lipped gash of a mouth spread in his most amiable smile, he inquired not after our health, as you might anticipate, but if we had "plenty sugar," for the Captain was an inveterate beggar. Telling him to come to the camp the next morning, we resumed our journey down the road, as we wished to camp a half mile below that evening. Before we could reach this point we had to cross a rushing creek two or three times. It was with difficulty that we persuaded the burros to make the crossing, and when they did go it was with a violent scramble for the opposite shore. We wondered many times how our plates were faring.

Havasu, or Cataract Creek, is a beautiful stream amid wildly picturesque surroundings. Havasu, freely translated from the language of these natives, signifies "blue water," and when combined with "pai," meaning people, gives them the very poetical name by which they are known—the People of the Blue Water. Havasu Creek is formed by the sudden appearance above the earth of an underground stream; the exact location of its emergence changing from time to time, but always within a small radius a short distance above the village.

Many miles above this place, at a point where caves and sunken rocks make an opening, the water can be heard far below the surface, rushing through its underground channel. The water is heavily impregnated with mineral—magnesium, lime, and silicate—which are deposited on everything it touches. Small twigs are surrounded with a cream-colored coating an inch or more in diameter; delicate ferns and moss still show their green under newly formed coverings of semi-transparent alabaster.

In many places a temporary barrier has caused the water to pause in its headlong flight; then, coral like, it proceeds to build higher and higher, forming 100-foot precipices, over which it hurls itself. Enormous stalactites hang suspended underneath a sheen of water, giving the whole scene a beautiful, withal a most unreal, appearance.

BRIDAL VEIL FALLS

Such a fall occurred just above the place we camped that evening. Some one, wishing to be entirely original, had named it the "Bridal Veil Falls" (see page 2). At the village above, the walls were 3,000 feet high and about half a mile apart, leaving a fertile bottom to the canyon. At this first fall the walls narrowed until they were scarcely a hundred yards apart at the bottom, the lower walls going up sheer. Large cottonwood trees were scattered over the bottom; ferns and moss clung to the moistened walls, and the wild grape-vine entwined itself over everything within reach. We felt well repaid for our two days of hard work to reach this lovely place; the most beautiful lateral canyon of all those that enter into the Grand Canyon.

It had been a fatiguing journey to reach this camp, which would be our headquarters for the next few days. Feed for the animals had been scarce, and the one little spring of water found at the head of the trail above the village was disgusting. "Topocobie," the Indians call it, the equivalent of "bad water," which it certainly was. Even the burros sniffed suspiciously at it. The half-decayed carcass of a horse, which had been shoved off the trail above, did not add to the general beauty of the locality.

Our camp here at the bottom was all the more enjoyable for this reason. The burros were now in clover, or at least in grass, up to their knees. Also they were sure of a three or four days' rest, for they could not be taken any farther, and it was up to us to do the hard work. The Indian agent had given us the keys to some buildings at this place, telling us that we could safely store our belongings therein while we were absent.

Our material was placed inside, but we preferred to sleep outside on the dry ground.

PHOTOGRAPHING AN INDIAN

Early the next morning Captain Burro dropped in for his promised sugar, and any other little gratuity we should care to add. We bribed him to pose for us while we made a photograph. On a similar occasion, several years later, on his offering to allow us to make his picture, we informed him that we wanted him in Indian clothes such as he used to wear long ago. He was on hand the next morning, ready for the picture. It was a chilly September morn, and the mist rising from the falls gave him an uncomfortable shower bath (see page 2).

The remainder of this first day was spent in exploring the wonders near at hand. A deep inner canyon entered on the right of the falls, with walls about 300 feet high, very narrow, and straight as a well. It is reported that the Indians formerly cremated their dead, together with all their belongings, on the cliff above, then threw their ashes into this canyon. Numerous tunnels and prospect holes were bored into its sides. Many years before great quantities of lead and silver ore had been mined and packed out of this place. In more recent years another company was organized to prospect the canyon for platinum. This company built the houses we had entered the night before.

A DANGEROUS WATERFALL

A mile down the canyon was another fall, even higher than the first, being credited with a drop of over 180 feet (see page 5). It was 30 feet wide, the water going over in a solid wall, not spreading, as did the upper fall. The first party of miners met with a fatality here, one of their number, Mooney by name, losing his life by the breaking of a rope with which he was being lowered to the bottom of the falls. The mining company had provided a passage around the falls in a spectacular manner. A sloping cave in the travertine, or deposited mineral, had been enlarged, and a winding stairway was hewn out of its sides. In two places an opening had been made in the sides, allowing a view of the falls. These openings were spacious, and compared well with a box in a theater. Large stalactites hung pendant from the walls, and gave the whole scene an enchanting appearance.

A short distance below the fall an iron ladder was erected 200 feet up the side of the wall, leading to a cave, which had been enlarged by the miners. It was held by spikes inserted into holes drilled into the walls, then wedged with wooden pegs. We had a creepy feeling when one of these allowed the ladder to swing outward a few inches as we climbed it.

MOONEY FALLS IN HAVASU CANYON: CATARACT CREEK
The falls are about 180 feet high and are built up by a mineral deposit from the water (see text, page 4).

THE INDIAN AT HOME

We visited the Indian's homes where we thought we were welcome. Their houses were merely a few logs leaning together, overlaid with willows, and with a covering of red earth over all. We saw a few fig trees and many apricot and peach trees. Some of the latter were in bloom, for this was the month of May. At one place we found a very old blind squaw, alone

LOOKING ACROSS THE COLORADO RIVER
FROM THE MOUTH OF HAVASU CANYON: CATARACT CREEK

The high water of the river has dammed the smaller stream into a long, deep pool. The line of division between the muddy and clear water can be plainly seen in the picture (see text, page 29). Note the barrel cacti growing on the rocks in the upper right-hand corner.

THE MOUTH OF HAVASU OR CATARACT CREEK AT LOW WATER

Note boats at the river's edge. Taken on the river voyage during a low stage of water. Compare this view with that of the same point when the floods fill the banks, shown on the following page.

THE MOUTH OF HAVASU OR CATARACT CREEK
AT THE JUNCTION WITH THE COLORADO RIVER AT HIGH WATER

Note the figure of a man on shore. This picture was taken during the flood stage on the Colorado and shows the water 60 feet higher than in the preceding picture. The walls in the distance are 4,500 feet high; those in the foreground are over 2,000 feet high. There would have been small chance for escape by climbing up such walls as these if our boats had been lost or injured beyond repair.

THE WEDGED ROCK

Found on the Bass trail on the north side of the Grand Canyon. The boulder has become loosened from the slopes far above, rolled down and lodged in the narrow gorge. Others of a similar nature are found within a few minutes' walk of this spot. Note human figures (see text, page 15).

THE GRAND CANYON AS IT APPEARS ON A CLEAR DAY (SEE ALSO TEXT, PAGE 17)

except for her dogs. She was busily engaged in carrying some corn from one building to another, guiding herself with a rope tied between the two structures.

Several years after this visit a cloudburst at the head of the canyon caused a number of storage dams to give way, the waters sweeping down through the unfortunate village. This helpless old woman was drowned, and nearly every house in the place was washed away. This fact is merely noted in passing, because it gives some idea of the violence of the storms which sometimes occur in this country.

The following day we prepared for the hard trip to the river, 6 miles below our camp. First we loaded our plate-holders, using one of the tunnels for a dark room. We have seldom had a better one. Then, with our cameras, food, and equipment packed on our backs, we set off down the canyon. As we descended, the walls grew higher and closer together; the stream had increased in volume until it was more like a small but turbulent river; the foliage everywhere blocked our path. We had to cross the stream several times. At times we would attempt to walk on the mineral deposit. Often this would crumble under our feet and we would be

THE GRAND CANYON FILLED WITH CLOUDS
This photograph was taken from the same point as the preceding picture.

plunged into the deeper water, our cameras being saved by holding them above our heads.

After about five miles of such traveling, the lower walls, which were about 200 feet high at our camp, now towered above us to a height of 2,000 feet; then they sloped back and up again to a total height of 4,500 feet. When we finally reached the river (see page 7) we found that much the same condition obtained there, the walls directly above the river being almost sheer for 2,500 feet, with only a ledge or two to break their sides (see pages 7 and 8). We afterwards discovered the trails of mountain sheep on these ledges.

DETERMINING AVENUES OF ESCAPE

In all our excursions to distant parts of the Grand Canyon we always endeavored to reach the river and locate these possible avenues of escape from it, for some day we intended to descend the stream in boats, as Major Powell had done in 1869-'71, and our knowledge of these places might prove to be valuable.

We were two weary but happy travelers when we dragged our feet into camp that night. The distance traveled was scarcely more than 12 miles; but it was 12 miles of tangled grape-vines, fallen boulders, and cataracts—about as

THE GRAND CANYON FROM THE FOSSIL ROCKS

Note the tents, the white dots, just above the central rock, below shadow, are about 3,500 feet below the rim.

THE SAME VIEW OF THE GRAND CANYON FROM
THE FOSSIL ROCKS WITH A MANTLE OF SNOW AND CLOUDS

LOOKING DOWN INTO THE GRAND CANYON
FROM THE HEAD OF BRIGHT ANGEL TRAIL

Clouds hanging below the rim. No snow below the 2,000-foot mark. Bright Angel Creek Canyon in the center.

much as an ordinary person would care to tackle in one day.

NO ROYAL ROAD

There is no royal road for the person who would explore the canyon's hidden secrets. Enthusiasm in unlimited quantities is a most needful qualification—enthusiasm in spite of discomfort, fatigue, and toil—all to gain what may be a doubtful goal. Looking back over our 12 years of experience at our work, we do not remember having ever made an easy trip in the

canyons, unless we counted those made down the Bright Angel trail, beside our home, and we do not count those, for they can easily be done in one day.

After having satisfied ourselves with the beauties of Havasu (Cataract Creek), we prepared to return. We left the agency about noon. A cold wind was blowing up the canyon and it was raining a little. On top we could see that it was snow instead of rain. We had no desire to make the homeward trip through a snowstorm, as we were ill prepared for cold weather at that time of the year.

ANOTHER VIEW OF THE GRAND CANYON
FROM THE SAME POINT AS THE PRECEDING PICTURE

Snow has descended to the plateau. Clouds have lifted from the canyon. Bright Angel Creek Canyon in the center.

By the time we had climbed the 15 miles of trail it was quite dark, and 5 or 6 inches of snow, very wet and heavy, had fallen. The burros would have all the water they needed this trip. We imagined that if we could get away from the rim—as the canyon's edge is usually termed—that we might get out of the storm belt, for often these storms hover over the gorge and spread back but a short distance. It was 10 p.m. when we stopped—we could hardly say camped. The snow did thin out some, but still there was plenty, and the ground was very wet. We had been enjoying a month of fine weather previous to this trip, and a snowstorm that late in the season was entirely unexpected. There were no sheltering rocks; our two blankets made a very poor bed, and we slept but little that night.

On the following day, were it not for the storm we might have made a detour to the Bass, or Mystic Springs, trail, as we did on a later occasion. Three or four miles up this trail, which is one of the wonderful parts of the canyon, a great boulder, loosened from above, has fallen into a side canyon and lodged there close to the top (see page 9)—just one of

SNOW AND CLOUDS IN THE GRAND CANYON: FROM THE STUDIO

With the battleship *Iowa* nearly obscured. Compare this picture with those on pages 18 and 19; all three views are from the same point

the many things that go to make this section of the country something entirely out of the ordinary.

STORM AND ATMOSPHERIC EFFECTS IN THE GRAND CANYON

We walked most of the 30 miles covered the next day, for the roads were slippery and difficult for the animals; also it was the only way we could keep warm. It was nearly midnight when we reached home and hurriedly pulled the packs from the burros.

The pleasurable thrills we experienced the following day when we developed our plates more than made up for any discomfort we may have experienced. More than that, the great amount of moisture in the atmosphere had formed into clouds which collected in the canyon a thousand feet below the rim, filling it from bank to bank. It was a rare and wonderful sight. The rising sun tinting the tops of the billows made it look not unlike the whirlpool of Niagara, but on an immense scale. These clouds hung in a layer or stratum about 400 feet thick; above the clouds everything dazzled in the sunlight; underneath it was a cloudy day. About noon the clouds became heated; they rose and disappeared, collecting again on the following night (see pages 11 and 16).

These storm and cloud effects of the spring form some of the most interesting phases under which the canyon can be seen. A few hours after the sun comes up every vestige of the snow has disappeared; in two or three days the clouds lift and vanish, leaving a clear, blue sky, destitute of every vestige of a cloud. Even in midwinter much the same condition holds true.

It is not often that the snow descends below the inner plateau, as it is changed to rain as it drops to the lower altitudes. On rare occasions it has fallen to the river itself. The nights at such times are quite cold on top, the thermometer tarrying somewhere near the zero mark. The canyon is just as beautiful as before, but differently so.

THE EFFECT OF SNOW

The snow hangs in clusters on the trees and bushes; then the rocky walls and the peaks in the canyon change their coats of many colors for a robe of purest white. Every hint of mist or haze disappears from the gorge below. The distant views of the mountains and canyon walls, ever deceptive in this rarefied atmosphere, are brought unbelievably near; the opposite wall of the canyon, although many miles away, looms directly before us (see pages 14 and 15). All is quiet and impressive; a junco flits across our path; a nut hatch taps on cedar or piñon, but beyond that there is no suggestion of life or motion.

Equally as interesting but of an entirely different nature, are the rains of July and August. These storms are quite often local— sharp, quick thunder storms—coming from one cloud; or it may be a cloud-burst a half mile away, while the sun continues to shine in other sections of the canyon. The preparations for these storms are often spectacular. The hour, we will say, is noon, with the sun shining directly against the north wall—the most uninteresting time of the day. The sky is cloudless—an infinite space of deepest blue; the heatwaves shimmer from the rocks.

Suddenly from below the horizon a round, white cloud pops up. Pops is the right word, for a minute ago it was not there. It is not part of the sky behind it, but hangs suspended like a great balloon, or a circle of white mosaic against a blue background. Others then appear, these last being shoved up by a great thundercap, snowy white above, black and forbidding beneath.

Then, like a flying squadron these clouds go sailing across the sky. Other clouds have appeared from nowhere in particular; they merge and spread, darkening and drifting over to the north (see page 18).

There they rest, for the north side is from 1,000 to 1,400 feet higher than our 7,000 feet elevation, and they seem to have reached their destination.

THE STORM KING REIGNS

A boom of distant thunder rolls up the canyon, losing itself in the many side gorges. A little feathery rain breaks from one end of the clouds, but rises again in mist before it reaches the lower altitudes. Jagged streaks of lightning pour from the clouds and the storm spreads. Thunder crashes as though the cliffs themselves were falling, the echos continuing to reverberate long afterward. Then the rain begins in earnest.

In a half hour the walls are deluged and angry; red-colored streams run off their sides.

STORM ON THE NORTH SIDE, WITH SUNSHINE IN THE CANYON

The small white spots in lower right corner are tents, 3,200 feet below. The nearest point on the opposite rim is 8½ miles distant (see also pictures on pages 16 and 19).

Waterfalls, the color of blood, pour from the plateau into the river over a thousand feet below. A glance through the telescope reveals a mad, foaming torrent hurling logs down the beautiful Bright Angel Creek of an hour previous.

In a short time the storm has passed, to break out anew in some other spot. The sun, even if it has been obscured temporarily, now comes out again. Rainbows appear double, and even triple in the gorge beneath. The moisture, rises in the form of vapor; collects in a cloud which hugs the higher peaks, or drifts in long strings when they strike the cooler air strata.

An Arizona electrical storm at night is a sight long to be remembered. Our little studio is so favorably located that we look into the very depths of the gorge, and can view these effects without being exposed to their fury. Many times we have worked from our veranda, exposing plate after plate in trying to record the electrical flashes. They are often disappointing; sometimes the flash will divide the plate entirely in two, beginning and ending out of the range of the plate or on either side of the angle of the lens. We also find that a single flash seldom brings out the formations in the canyon as

AN ELECTRICAL STORM AT NIGHT IN THE GRAND CANYON

The pictures on pages 16 and 18 are all of the same peaks, seen under different atmospheric conditions.

we want them to show in the printed picture. Our most successful pictures have been made by exposing the plate about one minute, thereby getting the benefit of the flashes of heat lightning as well as those of the stronger electrical flashes, the two combined giving us the illumination we want.

The account of our trip to Cataract Canyon, briefly detailed, gives an idea of our methods of reaching the little-visited portions of the canyon. We usually use burros in preference to the faster animals, because they are well adapted to the photographer's needs. We nearly always walk, but if we do ride or drive it is only on the level roads away from the canyon edge. The burro is quite easy to care for in sections where there is little feed; they get along on very little water, and our photographic material comes home in much better condition than when packed on a horse or mule.

When any climbing has to be done, the burros are hobbled in the best grass available and are left to shift for themselves until we return. If this happens to be on the inner plateau, we often find that they have made the acquaintance of wild burros, hundreds of which have their homes in the Grand Canyon. These wild burros are descended from a few which gained their freedom from some of the prospectors who were in this region twenty years or more ago.

OLD PROSPECTORS' TRAILS

At this point we might also remark that all completed trails leading to the bottom of the Grand Canyon were originally constructed by these same prospectors, or miners. They led to places that gave promise of developing into valuable mineral properties. In a few cases the miners realized something from their experimental work; in other cases they were doomed to disappointment.

When travel ceases over a trail it soon washes out, and only a slight trace remains after a few years of neglect. This is true of the French or Tanner trail, the original Hance trail, and in a greater or lesser degree of one or two others.

The one notable exception to this rule is the Cameron or Bright Angel trail, the only trail over which there is any continuous travel. A toll of $1 per animal is charged by the county, which looks after the upkeep of the trail; and as there is a total of 7,000 people yearly who make the journey on muleback, it has been changed and repaired until it is well-nigh perfect. It is so favorably located that it is less than seven miles in length, yet it reaches the river without any alarming grades, such as are usually found on mountainous slopes.

There are signs of ancient Indians at every point where it is possible to scale the sides of the canyon, these natural breaks being separated from each other in nearly every case by many miles of unscalable walls. We have, however, yet to see any evidence of an Indian trail that a horse could be taken over. They did not understand the use of explosives, and no trail to

the bottom of the canyon can be made without a liberal and intelligent use of giant powder, aided with pick and shovel. The remnants of these washed-out trails, crude as they are, aid us greatly when we wish to reach the distant and unexplored sections of the canyon and its tributaries.

II
THE CATARACTS OF THE LTTTLE COLORADO

THE oldest, least known, and in many ways one of the most interesting of the trails that lead into the great water-hewn chasm is that known as the French, or Tanner, Trail, located about 15 miles below the mouth of the Little Colorado River, which marks the beginning of the Grand Canyon. Just when this trail was first worked, and by whom, it is difficult to state. There is no doubt that it was opened by some of the earliest Mormon pioneers who had settled in the country adjacent to southern Utah previous to the time when John D. Lee took up his residence at Lee's Ferry at the beginning of Marble Canyon, some 65 miles above the canyon of the Little Colorado (see page 22). F. S. Dellenbaugh, in his interesting story of Major Powell's second exploration in 1871, records the fact that they found an abandoned log cabin built close to the river's edge even at that early day. This undoubtedly had been built by some of these adventurous pioneers.

A few miles above is a prominent ledge containing copper and other ores of more or less value, but sufficiently interesting to a mineralogist to induce farther prospecting. The Mormons have many tales of the nuggets of gold that John D. Lee brought from his hiding place in the canyons, and even today the hunt

ON THE TANNER TRAIL, AT THE BOTTOM OF
THE BLUE LIMESTONE OR MARBLE WALL (SEE TEXT, PAGE 26)

OUR TRAIL TO THE CATARACTS OF THE LITTLE COLORADO

Note figures of man and burro on top of ledge, which is 400 feet above the river (see text, page 28)

goes on for this mine, which may or may not exist. Our interest in the early history of this trail is merely passing; what did interest us was the fact that we had been told that it was still possible to get animals over the trail, and even to follow up the gorge itself to the mouth of the Little Colorado.

So thither we went one day in May, for we had heard rumors of photographic possibilities in that section; besides, we needed a change, and we always look on these journeys, hard as they usually are, in the light of a vacation.

VIEWED FROM THE CANYON EDGE

Before descending the trail we skirted the edge of the canyon to a vantage point known as Desert View. What a stupendous view it was! Owing to a bend in the gorge, there is more of the Grand Canyon visible from this point than from any other single view.

Far to the west we could see the top of the canyon wall where it makes its northern turn close to Havasu Canyon. Seventy miles of river lay coiled up in that one view, yet so fully was it hidden that we only caught a glimpse or two directly in front of us. Still beyond that farthest wall were the volcanic cones of Mt. Trumbull, Mt. Dellenbaugh, and others. Directly across the canyon was Cape Final, the extreme end of Greenland Point, that 20-mile-long peninsula which extends into the canyon from the north. To our right we could look into the very mouth of the Grand Canyon, and on past into Marble Canyon as well. Over to the southeast, and considerably below us, stretched the Painted Desert, brighter in color than the canyon itself, slashed through with the deep, narrow gorge of the Little Colorado. Beyond that stretched the Vermilion Cliffs, the wonderful fault or fold which crosses the Colorado River—visible from this point even to the head of Marble Canyon—while farther yet, 120 miles away, Navajo Mountain raised its rounded dome above the desert. The Coconino forest to the south ended only when the San Francisco peaks hid them from view.

The mere cataloguing of figures, however, gives no idea of the canyon. No description will make another see the subtle, elusive colors, as they shift and change with each hour of the day; no word picture will make another feel the dizzy heights, the sublimity, and the grandeur of it all.

On returning to the trail, after caching some of our provisions under a rock to save unnecessary packing, we each placed a 25-pound pack on our own backs, and with our bedding and provisions on Jennie, we set off down the trail. The upper wall of limestone, seldom very precipitous, was soon above us, the cross-bedded sandstone, which usually presents an unbroken face over 400 feet high, was broken here, so that it was no more difficult than the wall above it.

ROCK FORMATIONS

The rock formations in all parts of the Grand Canyon down to the inner plateau are almost identical. The two formations already mentioned have an approximate width of 1,000 feet, the upper slope being covered with scrubby trees, cedar, and piñon pine wherever they can find a footing. These walls vary in color from a chalky white to a rich cream or buff. Next in order comes the red sandstone, a sloping wall of rock over 1,000 feet in thickness. This wall is seldom very difficult to climb.

Of similar color on the surface is the next drop, a sheer wall of limestone, about 700 feet thick, and the hardest formation in the canyon.

THE CATARACTS OF THE LITTLE COLORADO
The figure of a man by the last drop gives an idea of their height (see text, page 20).

A LEAP IN THE INTEREST OF ART: NOT AS DANGEROUS, HOWEVER, AS IT LOOKS.

The red color in this limestone is only a stain from the sandstone above, and when broken it has a light-blue tint. Major Powell called this the marble wall, for he found it changed to marble in certain sections of the canyon which bears that name. This wall and the cross-bedded sandstone above are the two formations which present a problem to the climber or trail builder. In nearly every case where there is a trail the builders have taken advantage of a fault or displacement of rock; but these faults are few and widely separated.

Under the limestone is a bed of soft shales, 500 or 600 feet in thickness, a dark olive green in color, a covering of sage and cactus changing its hue but very little. The inner plateau, of

A MOUNTAIN SHEEP ON THE RIM OF THE CANYON: PHOTOGRAPHED BY A TOURIST
This photograph prompted us to follow his trail over a series of ladders known as the Humming-bird trail (see page 27).

which we have made previous mention, rests on this formation. It varies from one-fourth of a mile to several miles in width, depending on the locality. Nearly all of the temples or peaks in the canyon rise from this base. With the exception of the little strip of canyon adjacent to the Tanner trail (see page 21), any canyon below the shale is quite narrow and very precipitous. This deep, narrow section is known as the Granite Gorge, perhaps the wildest and most forbidding part of the Grand Canyon. All the upper rocks are stratified and almost uniformly level, but this lower gorge is twisted and turned in every direction (see page 33). This granite is capped with a 200-foot wall of sandstone, a hard conglomerate rock which often overhangs the granite; another very difficult formation to pass except where intermittent streams have broken it down.

PAGE FROM A GEOLOGIST'S DIARY

We had neither of these two formations at the Tanner trail, for here was the one notable exception to all this uniformity. Underneath the green shales we find an immense deposit of algonkian, which, we are told, is the earliest form of deposited rock. This section, or page it might be termed, seems to hold more of interest for the geologist than any other portion of this remarkable geologic book.

We had no particular difficulty in making the descent to the river, where we camped for the evening.

A SERIES OF LADDERS PLACED BY MINERS MANY YEARS AGO
MADE THE HUMMINGBIRD TRAIL UP THIS 420-FOOT WALL

The ladders are now badly decayed and the trail no longer used. The mountain sheep actually climb these walls.

On resuming our trip the following morning, we found enough difficult trail to make up for our brief respite. In low water it would have been possible to follow along the river's edge, but the spring flood was on at this time, and that road was blocked. No trail had been constructed above the river on the steep slope; but the numerous wild burros which roamed over this section had worn many little trails which went nowhere in particular, but crossed and recrossed each other in endless confusion. One of us would go ahead and figure out the best road, then the other would drive the burro up, scrambling and tumbling over the fallen boulders.

After four miles of such traveling we reached an abandoned miners' camp on a level spot below a perpendicular cliff. Directly above the camp an enormous section of the cliff was separated fron the main wall and leaned forward, hanging over the camp like the sword of Damocles, ready to fall any minute, so it seemed to us—a most uncomfortable place to camp.

The miners had tunneled into the walls in two or three places on both sides of the river, none of the tunnels being more than a hundred feet in length. A stream issued from each of the tunnels stained with copper and smelling strongly of sulphur. These claims are still held, and a certain amount of development work is done each year by two or three parties from the Utah side.

A TEST OF NERVE

From this point on to the mouth of the Little Colorado we slowly worked our way over one of the worst trails we have ever seen. The walls rose sheer above the river for 300 or 400 feet, then broke for a short distance into a steep slope, boulder strewn and cut up with many gullies. Above this slope was another perpendicular wall (see picture, page 22); 400 feet below roared the river. In two places large boulders all but blocked the trail. The burro, with her light but bulky pack, was very much frightened, and instead of swinging clear of the rocks, as they usually do, would shun the edge and catch the pack on the rocks. Twice she would certainly have gone over but for our assistance. One of us would lead, holding the rope close to the burro's head, while the other stayed behind hanging onto the pack harness, now shoving out a little to keep the pack clear of the obstruction, now pulling with all our might when it would catch and the burro would struggle to free herself.

All this time we were carrying our own loads except when we laid them aside to engage in this more difficult task. It was hot down in that narrow gorge, and while the river was just below us, it was out of reach, and we felt the need of water greatly before we got off the ledge of rock. The wall towered above us to a height of 3,200 feet; Chuar Butte, directly across the river, raised its level top to an equal height, so that we were in a canyon of that depth, and less than half a mile wide at the top. It was late in the afternoon when we dropped down off the ledge to the level of the river close to the mouth of the Little Colorado. This is the point where the gorge takes the name of the Grand Canyon; the section above, while nearly the same in appearance, is listed as Marble Canyon, for reasons previously given.

THE LITTLE COLORADO RIVER

An exclamation of surprise broke from us when we saw the Little Colorado. The water of the Colorado, now muddier than ever, and

50 feet above, the low-water mark, had dammed up the smaller stream into a deep, quiet pool half a mile or more in length. Its color was a deep indigo blue, and contrasted greatly with the water of the other stream. It is a pity that we have to record the fact that the water was strongly mineral and very unpalatable to the taste. The water in the Colorado, with all its mud and sand, was much preferable to it for drinking purposes.

We had been told of a small clearing a short distance up the canyon, and found it as described. A small level spot had been cleared of willows and mesquite, and had been cultivated at some time many years before. A small stone building, much resembling a cliff-dwelling, had been built under an overhanging wall. A plow had been packed in over this trail which we had found so difficult with our light loads. Cooking utensils and a coil of rope had been carefully concealed in a crevice in the rocks, then covered with sand and rocks. The wind, however, had blown enough sand away to reveal their hiding place.

A DECOY FOR A SETTLEMENT

It is quite likely that the person who had lived here was interested in prospecting, and was trying to raise enough vegetables for his own needs. Imagine living in such a place! Still it is not unusual to find men in these out-of-the-way corners of the West, happy and contented with their lot, diligently searching for the fortune which they feel sure they will find before another week has passed.

What a secluded spot it was! Nothing disturbed the utter stillness of the air. The sun sets early in these deep canyons, and the intense heat of midday had moderated somewhat. After locating our camp, we went down

to the river for a plunge, where our attention was called to a peculiar noise. We had seen many mountain-sheep tracks in this vicinity, and thought for a while that the noise was caused by a slide of shale, but we could not locate any movement.

Then Emery discovered what it was. On the opposite side of the pool the fins and tails of numerous fish could be seen above the water. The striking of their tails had caused the noise we had heard. The "bony tail" were spawning. We had hooks and lines in our packs, and caught all we cared to use that evening.

GILA TROUT

They are otherwise known as Gila Elegans, or Gila Trout, but "bony tail" describes them very well. The Colorado is full of them; so are many other muddy streams of the Southwest. They seldom exceed 16 inches in length, and are silvery white in color. With a small flat head somewhat like a pike, the body swells behind it to a large hump. Behind the dorsal fin, which is large and strong, the body tapers down slender and round, ending with a large, strong tail. They are nicely flavored fish, but are filled with countless small bones which divide and subdivide until they are almost like needle points.

As darkness settled over us that evening we began to wonder if our camp on the sand was to be as comfortable as we had anticipated. We had rejected the rock building as a sleeping place on account of the closeness of the atmosphere added to the fact that it was the home of innumerable rats. As the hour grew late the absolute stillness of the air of an hour previous changed to a violent wind which went tearing up the canyon, laden with sand from the shores of the Colorado. Instead of diminishing in fury,

HOW A DIFFICULT PHOTOGRAPH IS SECURED

This rather dangerous method was necessary to take the photograph on page 31, showing one mile of trail. Two ropes are used; one tied to a log, the other given one turn around the log. The operator sits in a loop in this second rope and is lowered to a ledge below, from which point the desired view may be secured. Then he climbs the rope which is tied, and the second rope is pulled in as it becomes slack. Thus the operator can rest when he becomes tired. The ledge in this case was 55 feet below. Had anything happened, the drop would have been about 300 feet.

THE FIRST MILE OF THE BRIGHT ANGEL TRAIL

The sheer wall covers the cherty limestone and the cross-bedded sandstone walls, 1,000 feet in thickness. The buildings on top, reading from the left, are El Tovar Hotel, the Bright Angel Hotel, and Kolb Brothers' studio, a little below the top of the canyon wall. The photograph was difficult to secure, and was taken as described on the opposite page.

HOW WE BROUGHT IN THE LUMBER TO BUILD A STUDIO IN THE CANYON

THE KOLB BROTHERS' STUDIO (LOWER RIGHT-HAND CORNER) AND
CAMERON'S INDIAN GARDEN IN THE CANYON, 3,200 FEET BELOW THE RIM

This shows the site of the Bright Angel trail from the rim to the plateau. It takes about 2¼ hours to make the descent to this point. The granite gorge, 1,300 feet deep, lies below the plateau (see page 26). The picture shows well the faulting of the rock near the top, where sections of the trail also may be seen.

THE BRIGHT ANGEL TRAIL FROM THE TOP TO THE BOTTOM OF THE CANYON

A more distant view than that on page 31, and showing the corkscrew route at the bottom in addition to that above the plateau. Close examination will show the Tonto trail on the plateau, to the right and left of the Bright Angel trail.

THE DEVIL'S CORKSCREW ON THE BRIGHT ANGEL TRAIL
This is in the granite gorge beneath the plateau, 4,000 feet below the rim.

as we had hoped it would, it kept increasing, coming first from one side, then from the other. We found that the junction of the canyons was the very center of the maelstrom of wind which poured in on us from all sides. The Painted Desert was directly above us, and it added it's quota of sand, as if we did not have enough already to contend with.

A REAL SAND STORM

We had seen sand storms before, but none to equal that. It literally rained sand from the desert above. Our camp articles, which had been carefully placed on shelving rocks, were blown helterskelter over the place; our bed, weighted down with stones, was the only refuge available, so we crawled into the blankets and covered up our heads, waiting for the passing of the storm. It is doubtful if the building could have been any more suffocating than our bed, covered up as we were. We both fell asleep after a while, and neither of us knew just when the wind ceased. When we awoke all was as quiet as before the storm.

The air, however, as is usual after these storms, was a brick-red color for two or three days.

We had long anticipated the next day's exploration. Prospectors had told us of having seen a series of cataracts about 15 miles up the river, but imagined that it was not possible to follow up the bed of the river, as they had only seen them from above. We were anxious to photograph the cataracts also, to learn if it was possible to reach them by the river. We had taken the season when the water was low on the Little Colorado for that reason. Loading ourselves with the inevitable cameras and plates, a lunch, and a large canteen of muddy water from the Colorado, we began our journey, starting at an early hour, for we were sure that

we had a hard day's work ahead of us. The burro was left to await our return.

A DANGEROUS TRAIL

The trip was somewhat easier than we had expected to find it; but it was hard enough, especially in spots. We took advantage of the shore wherever possible, sometimes finding long stretches of hard, firm sand on which we could make good time. It was quite different when we had to climb the canyon's sides, for the heat was intense when we got away from the river. Some of the sand, too, was very deceptive, and instead of being hard and firm, was treacherous quicksand. At times we spurted quickly over these places, resting on islands of solid rock, then would make another spurt. It would have been great sport but for the load we carried. In other sections we shunned the deposit entirely, for it was very soft and slippery, being about the consistency of slacked lime or of lard. We managed to pass it all, however, by crossing the stream two or three times, climbing the banks where it was possible, and taking advantage of the fallen rocks which lined the river's edge. About noon we reached the cataracts, which extended up the stream for half a mile or more (see page 40).

The canyon walls were very narrow here, and about 2,500 feet high.

We felt well repaid for our efforts. We not only secured our coveted opportunity, but had succeeded in doing what was commonly thought to be impossible. We went far enough above the ledges to find that it was entirely feasible to make our way still farther up the canyon, but time would not permit. We knew from the rock formation that we were within a mile of a spot we had previously visited on our initial trip into the canyon several years before. Were it not for the fact that we had a

THE GRANITE GORGE, 1,300 FEET DEEP

Composed of igneous rock. The granite is capped with a 200-foot layer of tonto sandstone. In many cases the granite can be climbed, but this upper cap overhangs for miles so that it is next to impossible to climb over it except where lateral streams have broken it down. The inner plateau, varying in width from a half mile to three miles, is directly above this tonto sandstone. Nearly all the temples, as they are called, rest on this formation. The granite extends nearly sixty miles in the first or upper part of the Grand Canyon, then disappears, emerging again near the lower reaches of the Grand Canyon. Some of the worst rapids we had to negotiate on the journey were found in the granite gorge (see also page 49).

RUST'S TRAMWAY, NEAR THE MOUTH OF BRIGHT ANGEL CREEK

The cable spans a 450-foot stream and the cage hangs about 30 feet above the water. Sightseers and hunters are taken across on this tramway to Rust's Camp, on Bright Angel Creek, and there outfitted for a trip into the Kiabab forest, on the north rim, where mountain lion abound. The nearest railroad is in Utah, over 200 miles distant.

burro and our camp to look after, we would have gone on up the canyon and climbed out as we did before.

III
SHOOTING THE RAPIDS
OF THE COLORADO

OUR photographic boating trip began September 8 at Green River City, Wyoming, where the U. P. R. R. crosses the Green River, hundreds of miles above our home in the Grand Canyon of Arizona.

A glance at a map of the Southwestern States (see page 56) will show our course down the Green and Colorado rivers. From Green River City, Wyoming, the river flows almost directly south for a distance of 60-odd miles; then turning directly east shortly after crossing the State line into Utah, it parallels the northern boundary of Utah and crosses into Colorado at the extreme northwest corner. This is the only point at which the Green River or its successor, the Colorado River, touches the State of Colorado. It is a common mistake to confuse the canyon of the Grand River in Colorado with the Grand Canyon of Arizona. After making a loop about 25 miles in length, the Green River returns to Utah, flowing in a general south-southwest direction through the eastern part of this State.

A MOUNTAIN LION

Captured by "Buffalo Jones" on the north rim of the Grand Canyon, packed by Dave Rust down Bright Angel Creek, across the river on the tramway, then up to the south rim on a burro. This lion afterward escaped in Las Vegas, Nevada, and ran through the main streets of the town.

CLEAR CREEK FALLS

These falls are close to 800 feet high, measuring from the cave from which they emerge to the bottom of the last leap. They are intermittent, running only about three months each year during the spring. A four days' journey was made to secure this one picture. The 1,300 foot walls of Bright Angel Canyon (see page 41) had to be climbed after a night spent in Rust's Camp. No load was carried except the cameras, provisions, and a little water. A deer trail six or seven miles long simplified the work of finding a way across the plateau. Then the walls of Clear Creek, equal in height to Bright Angel Canyon, were descended. The falls were reached after wading the stream for six or seven miles, and a picture secured as the shadows began to creep up the wall. Camp was easily made that night. There were no blankets; just a bed in the sand, beside a camp-fire of cottonwood logs and the yucca. The return journey to Bright Angel was made on the following day. While they can be seen from a distance and have been known for many years, the falls here have been visited by only this one party.

BRIGHT ANGEL CREEK

Looking toward the south wall of the Grand Canyon. This wall had to be climbed on the journey to obtain the picture of Clear Creek Falls shown on the preceding page.

READY TO EMBARK AT GREEN RIVER CITY, WYOMING, FOR THE 850-MILE TRIP
THROUGH THE CANYONS TO BRIGHT ANGEL TRAIL, IN THE GRAND CANYON

The wife and baby had been instructed to look for a signal fire in two months' time in Bright Angel Canyon (see text, page 73).

Four hundred miles below Green River City, at Blake, Utah, the stream is crossed by the D. & R. G. R. R. Between these two towns there is only one village on the river where provisions could be obtained. This was at Jensen, Utah.

WHERE RIVERS MEET

Over 100 miles below Blake, Utah, the Green River is joined by the Grand, flowing in from Colorado. These streams, combined, form the Colorado River. The Colorado River, running in a more southwesterly direction, crosses into Arizona, after about 150 miles in Utah. On being joined by the Little Colorado it changes its course and flows to the west, with many twists and turns. This is the section known as the Grand Canyon. Finally it forms the dividing line between Nevada and California on the west and Arizona on the east. It empties into the Gulf of California, in Mexico, about 100 miles from the U. S. line.

Five parties had made the entire trip from Green River, Wyoming, through all the canyons to Needles, California. The first was

FIRE HOLE CHIMNEY

One of the several butte formations found about 30 miles below the town of Green River, Wyoming.

Major Powell's world-famous exploration in 1869, supplemented by a second voyage two years later through all but about 125 miles of the Grand Canyon, where the second attempt was abandoned on account of high water.

The second complete trip was made by Nathan Galloway, a trapper and hunter, with a companion named Richmond, about 1891. The third was headed by Julius F. Stone, of Columbus, Ohio, accompanied by Galloway and two others. This trip was made in the fall and winter of 1909, the party leaving Green River September 12, just about two years before our own attempt. Two other parties had succeeded in making the journey through the Colorado

River canyons, starting at Green River, Utah. These are usually referred to as the Brown-Stanton party and the Russell and Monnette expedition. The parties that have failed to get through the first short canyons far outnumber those who have been successful.

RAPID-FLOWING WATERS

To get an idea of the descent of the Green and Colorado rivers, compare it with the St. Lawrence. From Lake Michigan to the Gulf this latter stream has a fall of 600 feet. This includes Niagara Falls, the Gorge Rapids, and many others. In an equal distance

THE OWNER OF THIS RANCH IN BROWN'S HOLE HAD BEEN MURDERED
AND HIS BODY SENT DOWN THE RIVER IN A BOAT
We found the door open and books, pictures, and furniture piled in the middle of the rooms (see text, page 49).

the Green and Colorado rivers fall 6,000 feet. Between the rapids there are many quiet stretches. These are formed by masses of falling rocks, which dam the river, or by lateral streams, which wash great masses of rock and debris into the stream during the flood stages. This often makes the water placid above; but quite as often the water pours over these barriers in a torrent.

The Green River townspeople came down to cheer us with tales of the others who had started out and were never heard from again. Several men, whom we had engaged to accompany us, from time to time, disappointed us when the time came to leave. The only one engaged who did show up was James Fagen, a

young man inexperienced at "roughing it," but strong, cheerful, and willing, and we were glad to have him along. We had wanted two assistants to help us with camp duties, photographic work, and in making portages around impassable rapids. With Major Powell's record of over 100 portages, we had some idea of the work ahead of us. To offset the handicap of our small party we had, however, the benefit of the experience of the others who had gone through before us.

Our boats, when loaded, weighed 1,200 pounds each, and looked like pretty big loads for one man to handle. The boats were flat-bottomed, but with considerable raise at either end. They were decked both bow and stern,

COTTONWOOD TREES ABOUT ONE FOOT IN DIAMETER
CUT DOWN BY BEAVERS (SEE TEXT PAGE 50)

with sealed air-tight chambers in each end. Our five cameras and a motion-picture camera were carried in these chambers; likewise, a month's provisions, photographic plates and films, and all necessary camp material. The oarsman sat in the open compartment, or cockpit, and the extra man on the deck behind.

FLAMING GEORGE, HORSESHOE, AND KINGFISHER

Though 16 feet long, the *Edith* and the *Defiance* looked small enough when compared with the width of the Green River when we started, for here it was 300 feet wide. We enjoyed ourselves thoroughly in the 60 miles of open country—hunting and fishing or listening to Jimmie's songs. He had a trained voice. His singing ceased for some reason or other shortly after we entered the canyons.

There were no rapids of consequence in the first three canyons—Flaming Gorge, Horseshoe, and Kingfisher Canyons—but our tranquillity changed shortly after entering Red Canyon.

The water was so low in Red Canyon that we struck many rocks, and we feared if this kept up that our boats would not last through the trip. Being built of cedar, less than half an inch thick, they cracked very easily.

In swift water, where there were few rocks, the boats were taken through in the usual manner, by pulling down stream; but when running bad rapids the order was reversed and the boats

REMARKABLE ENTRANCE OF LODORE CANYON

The river cuts directly through the mountains seen in the distance. One mile inside the entrance the walls are 2,700 feet high and nearly sheer (see text, page 51).

were turned with the bow pointing up stream. In this way we could see where we were going, and by pulling against the current the velocity was checked. The boats, being flat-bottomed and having considerable raise at either end, could be turned very quickly, and enabled us to pull from side to side and avoid the rocks ahead of us.

We had been informed before that some of these mountains were the hiding places of men who were "wanted" in the three States which bordered near here. Some escaping prisoners had also been traced in this direction; but all signs disappeared when the mountains were reached. We found several secluded cattle ranches in these upper canyons. The young men seemed to put in most of their time at hunting and trapping, and seldom went out without a gun. They had secured some wild cats, coyotes, deer, and an occasional mountain sheep.

ELLSWORTH KOLB ON LEFT AND EMERY KOLB ON RIGHT,
AFTER LESS THAN ONE MONTH ON THE RIVER

These fish—a catfish, suckers, and humpback, or bony tail—were found swimming on the surface of the water, being choked by the mud brought down by high water. They were struck with oars or caught with our hands in Lodore Canyon.

INNOCENT HORSE THIEVES

At one ranch we tried to buy some provisions. The men told us they would gladly supply us with what they had. In return they asked us to help them secure some of their horses from across the river, as their own boat had been taken out by high water. The horses were rounded up in a hidden valley, and were driven into the water ahead of the boat. After securing the horses, their welcome seemed to turn to suspicion, and they wanted to know what we could find in that wild country to interest us. We felt greatly relieved when we left them behind us.

"CAMP IDEAL": BELOW THE TRIPLET RAPIDS, IN LODORE CANYON
It is nearly impossible to describe the lonesome grandeur of this mighty canyon.

LOWER DISASTER FALLS, IN LODORE CANYON
Note how the river has cut in and is flowing almost entirely under the wall (see text, page 52).

Soon after emerging from Red Canyon into Brown's Hole we came to a deserted ranch. The doors were open; furniture, pictures, and books were scattered all over the place. We had previously heard reports of a murdered man's body having been found near here. I suggested to my brother that this might be his home; but we said nothing of this to Jimmie. Jimmie was worrying a good deal about our own troubles about this time.

Below this we found several other deserted ranches. On asking the few people we met the reason, they gave us evasive answers. Finally one man said that the country was infested with desperados and cattle thieves, and that a person had to be in with them or was not permitted to remain there. Our informant was there for some reason or other. We were told that the man at the first ranch had been murdered two years before; his body was placed in a boat and

NICE WORK AT HELL'S HALF MILE, IN LODORE CANYON

Sometimes it was necessary to change our plans instantly to avoid disaster, and rapid thinking was the order of the day (see text, page 55).

started down the river. We were also told that we were fortunate to get away from the ranch in the canyon with our valuables. The owner of this place had committed many depredations, and had served a term for cattle-stealing. Officers, disguised as prospectors, took employment with him, and helped him kill and skin some cattle. The skins, with the tell-tale brands, were then burned and buried. The officers turned in their evidence against him, and he was convicted.

This explained the strange actions of the men we had assisted. They thought we were trying a similar game. We had helped them steal eight horses and a colt ourselves!

In the lower end of Brown's Hole we saw a great many beaver and numberless cottonwood trees that they had cut down (see page

"HELL'S HALF MILE"

One of the most difficult rapids of Lodore Canyon, Colorado, on the Green River. Nothing but the motion picture gives any idea of the immense force of the water as it shoots out in a dozen different directions. The rapids increase in violence below this barrier. The slightest mishap here meant the destruction of the boat, at least, if not that of the party.

45). On two or three occasions our boats narrowly escaped splitting on snags of trees which they had buried in the river.

About the time we passed from Utah into Colorado a kind-hearted woman named Mrs. Chew informed us that they had a ranch at the other end of Lodore Canyon, which we were about to enter. She had a great fear of this short but dangerous canyon. Two of her sons had once attempted its passage. They lost their boat, and climbed out over the mountains, narrowly escaping starvation.

LODORE CANYON, N.W. COLORADO

Clouds had settled down into Lodore Canyon, and it was raining when we entered it. This canyon is the most wonderful example in the known world of a river cutting through a mountain (see page 46). The river was here first. An upheaval took place across its course, but so slow that the sand-laden stream sawed its way through the rocks, keeping its old level. When we were one mile inside the canyon, its walls towered over 2,000 feet above us.

A few miles further down is a rapid which Major Powell had named Disaster Rapid (see page 50). Here one of his boats, although made of one-inch oak, had been broken completely in two. We ran the upper part of this rapid, but found ourselves on some rocks below, and could not proceed on account of the low water. It was late and we had to camp on a low, rocky island that night.

The next day we proceeded to change our camp, running our camp material across on a trolley. The stream on this side, while small and rather shallow, was swift and difficult to cross. After all weight from the boats was sent across, we proceeded to line the boats across, two men working on shore with the lines while the other clung to the boat and maneuvered it. When ready to take the second boat across, the sun broke through for a short spell between the showers.

MAKING A MOTION PICTURE UNDER DIFFICULTIES

This was our chance to get a motion picture; so I set up the camera and went to work, while the others worked with the boat. I was paying little attention to what they were doing. Suddenly I heard a call, and on looking up saw that my brother had been carried from his footing and was being swept down the rapid. Jimmie had been holding the line on shore until the end was reached, then was instructed to go above to the crossing and join me. There was not a moment to lose. I caught up a rope and ran down the shore, reaching my brother, when a rock stopped the boat for an instant. That film was finished as he climbed out over the rocks.

It was fortunate he got out at this place. At Lower Disaster Rapid the stream almost disappeared under an overhanging wall (see page 49). A string, with one end attached to a rock and thrown from the shore to the wall, measured less than 25 feet. The remainder of the stream, which had been 300 feet wide in the flat country above, went under that wall.

DANGEROUS RAPIDS

The next day we were not so fortunate. The *Defiance*, as my brother's boat was named, was thrown on her edge on touching a rock, and was held there by the swift-rushing river. My brother saved himself by climbing onto the rock. I was having some difficulty in a whirlpool below and could not see him, but knew that something was wrong when a rubber bag containing a sleeping-bag came floating down the stream. Jimmie had waded out in a pool at the end of the rapid and saved the boat. Ellsworth was quite close to the shore, and we soon had a rope and life-preserver to him and pulled him to shore. Every plank on the bottom of the boat was split, and as I had received a similar upset that morning we pulled out on shore for repair. We had lost our two guns in the last tilt. They were too long to go under the decks. The cameras had all been in the muddy water, likewise our provisions. Some of our motion-picture film was lost. We placed all of our material on the shore to dry, as we were enjoying a brief period of sunshine.

But it was short, for a deluge of rain, driven by a heavy wind, came sweeping up the

END OF LODORE

Echo Cliffs, opposite the mouth of the Yampa River. This wall repeated an echo of a count from 1 to 7 when called from the shore of the Yampa. Note our boat under the cliff.

ANOTHER VIEW OF THE END OF LODORE CANYON
Mouth of the Yampa on the right. Walls are about 700 feet high. The trees are red cedar.

canyon. We put up a small silk tent and got everything inside; but it was long after midnight when we retired, after having repaired all possible damage. Landslides vied with the thunder, the wind, and the rain that night to add to our discomfort. And as we slept Jimmie rose up in his sleep and called, "There she goes over the rapids."

We awoke the following morning to find a 6-foot rise on the river. It was so muddy that fish were swimming on the top of the water,

gasping for fresh water. We secured 14 by striking them with our oars. When suckers and catfish come to the top on account of mud in the water it is pretty bad. A test of the water showed that it contained 20 per cent of an alkaline silt. Afterward we found many dead fish, with their gills filled with this mud.

We had suspected Jimmie of homesickness for some time. This day he told us his story. He had an invalid mother, and he had always looked after the needs of the family, aided by an older

THE END OF THE LABYRINTH CANYON, SHOWING THE BUTTES OF THE CROSS

These two formations are about half a mile apart, and the cliffs are about 700 feet high. Few people know that motor boats make the journey in perfect safety, starting from Green River, Utah, for 120 miles down to the junction of the Green and Grand rivers; also 40 miles up the Grand, in canyons 1,300 feet deep. There are no rapids in this section. This is only one of many hundreds of wonderful rock formations which are found in Labyrinth and Stillwater canyons.

brother. When the proposition of taking the river trip came up, serious objections were raised by the family; but when the ticket came he concluded to go, with or without their consent. Now he feared that his mother would not live, or that we would be drowned, and that he would be left on the shore and would be unable to get out. All this he told us with tears in his eyes. No wonder he felt blue.

We cheered him all we could, and told him we would send him out at the first opportunity.

RUNNING THROUGH LODORE

The last place of importance in Lodore Canyon had been named Hell's Half Mile (see pictures, pages 50 through 51). We thought it was all of that and then some. The entire stream was blocked by a lot of massive rocks, flung from the cliffs above in riotous confusion. This had happened at a point where the descent of the river was the greatest yet encountered. On the left side the barrier of

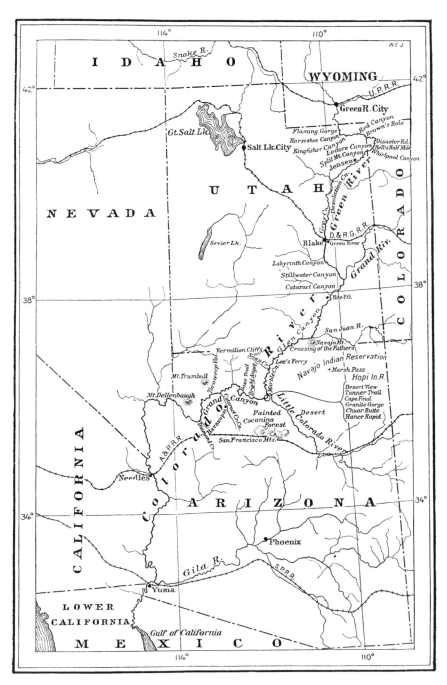

MAP OF GRAND CANYON FROM GREEN RIVER, WYOMING,
TO MOUTH OF COLORADO, IN MEXICO

rocks was crowned by a giant cottonwood once washed down on a flood, with its roots extending over the foaming torrent, which whirled and tore through every crevice between the rocks.

We carried all the weight from the boats high above the rapids, climbing over mud-covered boulders, dodging under scrubby trees, sliding down recently washed-out gullies, staggering under the weight of the loads. Many times we fell, bruising ourselves on the marble-like rocks. The recent rise in the river, which had now receded, had left a slime of mud over these rounded boulders. Our clothes were torn to tatters. It took 18 loads to empty the boats.

Carefully inflating our life-preservers and adjusting them, we then went to work on the *Defiance*. Our other experiences at working past difficult rapids were as child's play when compared with this. At first, where the rapid was less violent, we lined the boat from the shore, or I rowed, pulling upstream, dodging here and there, while my brother held the line on shore, dropping her down as each threatening rock was passed. We struggled to retain our footing when standing, waist deep, in the water below protecting boulders, as we lifted the stern over a submerged rock, then slid the boat forward (see pictures, pages 49 through 51); she would balance a moment, the bow would shoot into the air, then fall down with a thud and another rock was passed.

WHEN SECONDS COUNT

The slightest miscalculation would mean a wrecked boat; the least misstep would plunge us into the torrent. The life-preservers would have been of little use there. The rocks would soon batter one into insensibility. Even in less violent water the heavy sand collecting in the clothes soon sinks a swimmer, and a body once taken down in that manner seldom rises to the surface.

When we came to the barrier, we concluded the only way to pass this in safety was to nail skids to an upright log which we found wedged between two large rocks at the end of the cottonwood tree. Both the log and the tree seemed to have been placed there for our convenience. In all this work there was only room for two, so we made use of this opportunity to get a motion picture—the last we were to get with Jimmie's assistance. During the breathing spells we would look up and find he was forgetting to turn the crank. We would call to him, then all would go to work again. We kept the boat in the water as long as possible, its bouyancy helping a great deal, as we lifted only one end at a time. Again we lifted the stern of the boat, then threw the rope from the bow over the root of the tree and tugged away until she was balanced on the skids. She was slid carefully forward, tipped slightly, then with a rush like that of a vessel on a greased runway she shot into the pool below, almost breaking away into what remained of Hell's Half Mile.

At the end of Lodore Canyon we found a small cabin occupied by an old man. Rumor had it that he was living this hermit's life because he had engaged in a shooting scrape or two, and had been quicker than the other in pulling his gun. He was harmless enough when we found him, as he was feeble and childish. He had been in this section when Major Powell was making his survey, and had many interesting stories to relate of the early days. The disappointing thing about the stories was that he would never finish them, but would break off in the middle of his narrative and begin on something else.

What interested us all more than anything else was that the Chew ranch was on the plateau above. When we arrived we found that Mrs.

SCENE IN THE STILLWATER CANYON
The man is standing 1,300 feet above the Colorado River below (see text, page 61).

THE LAND OF STANDING ROCKS ABOVE
THE JUNCTION OF THE GREEN AND GRAND RIVERS

The rocks here are split and cracked in every conceivable manner. Some of the cracks were 300 to 400 feet deep. There was little or no vegetation. Apparently this condition extended for great distances in every direction across the Colorado; far away were great spires of rock looking like a city of churches. Stillwater Canyon (see text, page 61).

A TYPICAL RAPID IN CATARACT CANYON

This type of rapid was very common in Cataract Canyon. The river falls 75 feet in three-fourths of a mile in this section. Our boats were carried up on this rock, then reversed and whirled through the narrow channel on the right. The picture gives no idea of the drop or the violence of the water. There are records of nine parties who have lost their lives in this 41-mile canyon. If a boat is wrecked and the occupants are not drowned and succeed in climbing up the walls of the canyon, they find themselves in the desolate country of the Land of the Standing Rocks (see pictures, pages 58 and 59, and text, page 66).

Chew had crossed the mountains and joined her husband and sons. When she saw us she exclaimed "Why, boys, I thought you had passed here a week ago." It had taken us eight days to get through 20 miles in Lodore Canyon, so you know we had some trouble. The river descends 425 feet in that short canyon.

THROUGH EASTERN UTAH

The Chews said they were going to Jensen, Utah, 40-odd miles away, on the following day, and gladly agreed to take Jimmie along. We were going to the same place by river. We traveled through Whirlpool and Split Mountain Canyons in two days' time, just four hours behind Jimmie. We saw him off on the stage the next day, a very happy boy, bound for the railroad, 120 miles away. We sent some of our photographic material along with him, knowing it was in the best of hands.

Two more canyons—Desolation and Grey—had to be traversed before we reached the D. & R. G. Railroad. This is the point where Stanton and Brown, with their party, began their survey for a railway through the canyons of the Colorado. Mr. Brown and two of their companions were drowned in Marble Canyon above the Grand Canyon.

Stanton, undismayed by these reverses, re-outfitted with heavier boats and completed the journey to the tidewater. Later it was the starting-point of the prospecting expedition composed of three men—Russell, Monnette, and Loper. Records have been kept of nine other parties who have left this place for the passage through Cataract Canyon. Three men only escaped. The others simply disappeared.

LABYRINTH AND STILLWATER CANYONS

Few people know that parties are taken by motor boat down the Green River to its junction with the Grand, and part way up the Grand, and then by automobile to the railway. We have no doubt but that some day this will become a popular way of seeing these wonderful canyons. All element of danger from rapids is removed from this 150-mile trip. Some of the scenery en route might be compared to the Garden of the Gods, but on a scale a thousand times greater and a thousand times more picturesque (see pages 55 and 58).

At the junction of the Green and the Grand rivers we climbed out through a side canyon above Cataract Canyon. It was "The Land of Standing Rocks," a country split, eroded, and cragged in every conceivable manner. There was little soil and scarcely any vegetation. The weird solitude, the great silence, the grim desolation seemed to affect us here more than at any place on the trip. We could drop rocks into the crevices, and watched them disappear into the darkness far below us. On going to the edge, 1,300 feet above the Colorado River, we would find some of the rocks overhung 50 feet or more.

JUNCTION OF THE GREEN AND THE GRAND RIVERS

In Cataract Canyon's 41 miles there are 45 bad rapids, and there must have been at least that many men who have attempted its passage and were never heard from again. We know one man who did climb out after losing his boat and who existed for weeks on cactus and herbs until he was finally discovered. He is an able-bodied man today, but has practically lost his reason.

The Colorado River at this place was ten times greater than the Green in the upper canyons, and the rapids were correspondingly more dangerous. We were surprised to find here tracks of some person who was ahead of us.

That evening we caught up with the man who had made the tracks we had seen. He gave the name of Smith, admitted rather reluctantly that he was trapping, and did not appear greatly pleased to see us. Considering the fact that we were 150 miles from the last habitation, this struck us as being rather strange.

GOING IT ALONE

It was too late to go any farther that evening; so, as there was plenty of room, we camped below him and invited him over to share our evening meal. After dessert, which happened to be some pineapple which we had kept for some special occasion, he became more sociable. He had started from Green River, Utah, one month before, he told us. He had an old rotten boat that one good wave would knock to pieces. He had made no attempt to run any of the twelve rapids we had passed that day, but held his boat with a chain and worked down in that manner. Once he had been dragged into the river, twice the boat had been upset; he was engaged in drying out his

ANCIENT PICTOGRAPHS IN GLEN CANYON

Note the mountain sheep on the arrow. The figures near the center may represent a dance somewhat similar to the masked dances of the Hopi. The large figures on the left, we are told, represent a stone last on which they wove a sandal. The spiral indicates water. The quiet waters of Glen Canyon were quite a rest after the torrents above. We found here many evidences of ancient Indians, who had reached the river through the side canyons.

tobacco when we found him. This was the only thing that seemed to worry him. He seemed to have no idea of the country below, but thought it was getting better. We told him what we knew of it, and on the following morning, offered to take him through with us and help him with his boat, but he declined. It almost seemed like suicide to us. On parting he promised to write to us if he ever got out of Cataract Canyon.

As we proceeded on our journey we wondered more than ever if he had not made a serious mistake in attempting it alone. The rapids increased in violence and frequency; the walls drew closer together and towered above us until they were over 2,000 feet high; there was small chance to climb out. At one point the river descended 75 feet in three-fourths of a mile. We had so many narrow escapes ourselves as we ran these rapids that we temporarily forgot all about Smith and his troubles.

DARK-ROOM DIFFICULTIES

We put up our small tent and camped at one place for two days, not only because I was not feeling well, but we wished to develop some plates and films as well. For this work our dark room or tent, was hung inside the other tent, and we proceeded with our work just as though we were at home—300 miles below us. We settled the mud in a bucket of water by placing the bruised leaf of a prickly pear cactus in the vessel. A substance which oozed out settled the mud and made the water sufficiently clear to develop our plates. A hole dug in the sand at the side of the river gave us water for cooking purposes, nearly as clear and in greater quantities than the method first mentioned.

Rapid number 23 was just below this camp; it was one of the biggest drops of any in that section. We made moving pictures of each other in turns as the boats reeled and plunged over the cresting waves. We each had an extra oar knocked from our boat in this rapid, but recovered them a mile down stream in a whirlpool.

PHOTOGRAPHING AN UNRULY SUBJECT

The walls increased in height until they towered nearly 3,000 feet above us, the left wall being nearly perpendicular. To prevent our minds from dwelling too much on the dangers which surrounded us, we proposed having a little sport. The two boats were placed stern to stern and lashed together. My brother sat in the first boat and rowed down-stream. I sat on the deck behind with my legs wrapped around the bow, holding the moving-picture camera down with my chin, turning the crank with my right hand, and clutching at the hatch cover with my left hand. In this way we passed over two small rapids. My brother said that the best picture would have been of myself as I rode the bucking boat over the turbulent water. This method was never tried when in the larger rapids.

The last rapids in Cataract Canyon were the worst of all in some respects. The walls went sheer from the river on one side, the shore had almost disappeared from the other. Great boulders had dropped down and blocked one side of the channel. Twelve-foot waves overtopped and threatened to engulf us as we rowed into this rapid, carefully pulling away from the dangerous places.

But one danger was no sooner avoided than another jumped up before us. In the last rapid the shores disappeared altogether. An island lay in the middle of the rapid, but the stream on the left was entirely blocked with rocks. The white water swept under the right wall until it surged into a lot of fallen rock; then it crossed to the opposite side and swept it clean. The rapid was much in the shape of the letter S.

We rowed into this without stopping to look it over. First we pulled against the current, keeping close to the island, matching our strength and skill with the water which tried to drag us into the turn. This danger past, we pulled across the swift-running center, 6 or 7 feet higher than the water along the shores; then the opposite side was avoided in the same way, and we landed, breathless, on a shore below the rapid and proceeded to bail out with a grocery box which we kept under the seats.

Then our thoughts reverted to Smith. What would he do when he came to this rapid? The only escape was a narrow, sloping ledge beginning some distance above the rapid and reaching a height of 60 or 70 feet above the water at the lower end of the rapid. It would be possible for him to climb over this with his provisions, but the idea of taking his boat up there was entirely out of the question, and, poorly equipped as he was, an attempt to run it would only end in disaster. The breaking of an oar, the loss of a rowlock, or the slightest knock of his rotten boat against a rock, and Smith's fate

ABOVE THE SOAP CREEK RAPID, IN MARBLE CANYON
The scene of two of our upsets. Note figure on the right shore (see text, page 66).

A FALLEN ROCK IN THE UPPER PART OF MARBLE CANYON
Note the boat on the right-hand shore just emerging from behind a rocky point.

would be similar to that of others whose bones were buried in the sands.

OTHERS WHO HAVE TRIED

Below Cataract, in Glen Canyon, we came to the Hite ranch and post-office, the first sign of human habitation for 175 miles, since leaving Blake, Utah. Mr. Hite had kept a record of the parties who had attempted Cataract Canyon and were never heard from again. On one occasion a man staggered into his door and fell to the floor. He said his companion was drowned, and that he had eaten nothing for a week but a horned toad and a lizard. Whether this was true or not, he was in a critical condition, and it was some time before he was able to go out across the mountains. Hite promised to advise us if Smith ever reached there alive.

The quiet waters of Glen Canyon were quite a rest after the torrents above. We found here many evidences of ancient Indians, who had reached the river through the side canyons. We found several ruined cliff dwellings, with broken pottery and arrow heads scattered about. There were strange pictographs of masked figures and of deer and mountain sheep on the walls (see page 62).

Glen Canyon was filled with many curious rock formations, including arches and caves. It is in this vicinity that the natural bridges of southern Utah are found.

It is not far from this point that Rainbow Natural Bridge was recently discovered. We thought we knew where it was and searched long and earnestly for the side canyon, but we had passed it before starting to look for it. It was a great disappointment, for we had been told it was only six miles from the river. We consoled ourselves with the thought that we would make the journey overland at some later day to reach it.

PATHFINDERS

In the middle of Glen Canyon we came to an old ford, known as the Crossing of the Fathers. Early in the fifteenth century Spanish priests had taken the Indian trails leading to this ford and had crossed over into Utah. Thus this section was visited before the English settled on the James River; yet how much does the American public know about it today?

While climbing out here we heard some hammering and blasting, but we traveled 15 miles down the river before we discovered what had caused it. We saw the strange sight of a half-built steamboat in the mouth of a little side canyon, with cliffs rising six or seven hundred feet above it. Between 15 and 20 men were at work putting it together. This boat was to be used to carry coal and driftwood to a placer dredge working at the head of Marble Canyon, 20 miles farther down the river.

We reached the dredge that evening. This was at Lee's Ferry. Thirty-odd men were at work here, 120 miles from the nearest railroad. They shook their heads and told us of the great boulder-filled rapids in Marble Canyon, which they had seen from the cliffs above.

"GET THE PICTURE FIRST"

We had traveled less than one day below this place when we came to the famous Soap Creek Rapid (see page 64). It was just below this rapid that Mr. Brown had lost his life. My brother wanted to run Soap Creek Rapid, and suggested that I should make a motion picture as he came down, keeping a rope and life-preserver close at hand, so that I could run to the end of the rapid in case of an upset. His last instructions were: "If we upset, get the picture first."

I confess that I was shaking at the knees as he went back to prepare for the plunge.

THE SHEER WALLS OF MARBLE CANYON
The walls in the foreground are about 900 feet high; those in the distance are nearly 3,500 feet high.

A HUGE CAVE IN MARBLE CANYON
Compare with the figure of a man standing on right, near edge of the picture.

The rapid was a third of a mile long. I had set up the camera about 50 yards below the first dip. It seemed a long time before he came in sight above the rapid; but when once in its grip it was not more than a second or two before he was opposite me, pulling with every ounce of strength to avoid the one rock that blocked his passage.

For a moment it seemed that he would gain his goal; then the *Defiance* was lifted suddenly by an unexpected wave; she touched the rock for an instant and turned on her edge, then broke loose and turned upright again. The entire upset had occupied less than two seconds.

I lost sight of my brother when the boat went over, but felt reassured on seeing him hanging to the gunwale and climbing in again as the boat righted herself. He scrambled for the oars, and brought her around just in time to avoid being taken into a cresting wave. The filled boat had lost her buoyancy and struggled through the foaming water. Time and again she disappeared from sight, and I wondered if she would sink; but with the rhythm of a pendulum she rose each time she fell, getting smaller and smaller in the distance until the end of the rapid was reached.

"Did you get the picture?" This was my brother's question, and one which I found myself unable to answer. I knew that I had the start. I was just as certain that I had taken the long run after he had regained the oars, for I had carefully followed him, looking through the finder, but had no idea what I was doing when the boat upset.

My brother was still determined to run the *Edith* through, feeling sure that his first passage gave him the experience necessary to handle it successfully. I advised waiting until morning, for it was now getting late in the day; but he said "he would sleep better with the rapid behind us, instead of having to run it on the following morning, and with one boat below the rapid I could save him if it came to the worst."

While he walked back to the *Edith* I built a fire, then returned to my station in the *Defiance*. It seemed that he would never come. Finally he appeared above the rapid and paused an instant before making the plunge. It was now in the gloaming and this was indistinct, but I could make out that he had missed his channel and was carried into a vortex of contending waves. He disappeared for an instant, then the bottom of the boat, stern first, was shot out of the water and fell over, upside down. This was all I could see.

Boat and all apparently had disappeared. I launched the *Defiance* and waited. Soon a dark line appeared rising on the waves. It was the bottom of the *Edith*. I listened but if there was any call it was drowned in the roar of the water. The boat was gradually drawing nearer and I prepared to save her, having made up my mind that a dark object in the middle of the stream was my brother on a rock.

ACROBATIC PHOTOGRAPHY

Drawing close to the *Edith*, I heard a strangled call, and saw that he was hanging to the boat. A life-preserver was floating ahead of him and he was calling to me to save it. In a moment I was at his side and was pulling him into the *Defiance*. Then we caught the upturned boat just as we were carried into the next rapid, the rapid which had proved to be the last for Brown.

There was no time to turn the boat upright, so we held to the rope to save her as she dragged us on and on into the darkness. It was a hard pull, but I made it, and kept clear of the overhanging rocks under which the current ran. But the *Edith*, filled with water, kept us

AN AIR MATTRESS IN CONNECTION WITH A SLEEPING BAG GAVE US A LIGHT,
DRY, COMFORTABLE BED, EVEN ON WET SAND OR ROCKY, UNEVEN GROUND

from making the landing, and a mile of swift water was passed before we pulled into an eddy and tied the boats to a boulder.

The lower end of Marble Canyon held many curious grottos; in places the walls were honey-combed with caves. Some of these caves made excellent camping places, for the flood waters had been into them and had deposited a level floor of sand. Driftwood was piled up at the mouth of one of them, and a spring of water bubbled from the rocks not far distant. Although it was early in the afternoon, we could not resist this invitation to camp, for it was snowing on the heights above and a cold wind blew up the canyon. The only disturbing element at this place was the roar of another rapid just below.

When lying in our beds the noise made by the water was terrific, and we would imagine we heard all sorts of impossible things, such as crying children, women screaming, and the shrieking of the wind. On rising up in our beds it would once more be the roaring of the rapid. We could plainly hear the rolling of rocks as they turned over and thumped against one another.

The walls of Marble Canyon fell sheer for hundreds of feet in many places, the gorges at

IN LOWER MARBLE CANYON

Note the boat near the right side. A number of the rapids had no beach whatsoever on either side

We arrived at the end of Bright Angel Trail after two months and ten days on the journey through the canyons from Green River, Wyoming, a distance of 850 miles. "In five hours we had dropped 178 feet. We anchored under the tramway and prepared to go up Bright Angel Creek and build our signal fire. We had some doubts if the fire would be seen on top, for storm clouds filled the canyon; but now and then a rift appeared and we hoped they saw the light" (see text, page 77, and the next picture).

WATCHING FOR THE SIGNAL FIRE

Seventy days after leaving Green River, Wyoming, we built our fire in Bright Angel Creek Canyon, signaling our home, six miles distant, on the opposite rim of the canyon, that we would arrive the next day. The fire was seen the instant it was lit by Mrs. Emery Kolb and her daughter Edith. With the telescope, our two forms could be distinguished sitting by the fire six miles away.

LEAVING HOME A MONTH LATER TO FINISH OUR JOURNEY
DOWN THE CANYONS TO NEEDLES, CALIFORNIA

THE FIRST CAMP FROM BRIGHT ANGEL TRAIL WAS BELOW THIS SKELETON, WHICH WE HAD HELPED COVER UP FIVE YEARS BEFORE

The body was lying in a natural position, with no large bones broken. The pockets contained a Los Angeles newspaper dated 1900. There was nothing about the clothes by which he could be identified. Apparently he was a prospector.

ONE MILE ABOVE TAPEAT'S CREEK: PULLING AWAY FROM THE SHORE

Lauzon, "instead of walking around such rapids as he could while we ran the boat, would lie down on the deck, hanging on to the bulkhead like grim death as the great waves rolled over him. Then he would shake the ice-cold water from his clothes and with a grin would remark, 'Young fellows, wasn't that great!'" (see text, page 79). Our method in all rocky rapids was to drift down stern first, keeping the boat under control by pulling up stream or against the current. This gave the oarsman an opportunity to see what was ahead. The boats, being flat-bottomed and built with a rake or raise at either end, could be turned very quickly and pulled from side to side when rocks threatened.

these points being very narrow (see pages 67, 68, 71). In one place we recorded a high-water mark 107 feet above the low water on which we were traveling.

IN THE GRAND CANYON—
THE SIGNAL FIRE

One week after leaving Lee's Ferry we were at the Hance Rapid in the Grand Canyon. This was the beginning of the abrupt and violent rapids of the granite gorge. This rapid was run in safety, but not without some exciting experiences. Then came a series of rapids which differed from those we had found above. The rapids we had been traversing were usually caused by the debris from side canyons, which dammed the stream and transformed what might have been a good, swift stream with a continuous drop to a succession of mill ponds and cataracts. In most cases in the low water the deposit made a shore on which we could land and inspect the rapid from below.

RUNNING A TYPICAL RAPID OF THE GRANITE GORGE

Such rapids are one-third to one-half of a mile in length. One can hardly describe the sensation of being cata-
pulted along like a cannon-ball through such angry water.

But the rapids in the granite gorge were different. They were not caused by any great deposit of rock, but rather seemed to be formed by a single narrow dike or ledge, rising from the bottom. The rapids dropped almost like a dam, then tailed out in long lines of interference waves. Had it not been so cold, this style would have been more to our fancy. The descent was abrupt, but careful handling of the boat took us past every danger. There was little chance to make a portage in any of those rapids had we desired to do so, which we did not.

We gave them but a glance, then rowed into them. One had a fall little short of 35 feet. The next was even more abrupt, and dropped about 30 feet. We paused only to bail out after each rapid, then pulled on again.

In five hours we had dropped 178 feet. We never paused in our rowing until we anchored under the tramway, and prepared to go up Bright Angel Creek and build our signal fire.

THE HERMIT CREEK RAPID, IN THE GRANITE GORGE
The wave on the right side is 15 feet high. Two parties have lost boats in this rapid.

When our last letter was sent out we had told them to begin to look for us about the fourteenth of November; it was now the sixteenth. We had some doubts if the fire would be seen on top, for storm-clouds filled the canyon; but now and then a rift appeared, and we hoped they saw the light.

Ragged and tired, but happy, we climbed the trail the next day to meet with a reception that repaid us for all we had undergone. They were on the job, and saw the fire as soon as it was built.

One month later, or on December 19, we were ready to resume our journey (see page 74).

It was with no great amount of enthusiasm that we left home to finish the trip to Needles, California. Nearly a foot of snow had fallen, and had, drifted over the side of the canyon. The snow had descended to the plateau, 3,000 feet below something unusual, occurring only after several nights of zero weather on the rim. A little thin ice covered the pools at the river's edge.

A RECRUIT JOINS US

With us was a new man who was anxious to make the trip—Mr. Bert Lauzon. Lauzon was a practical miner and a cowboy as well—an

GRANITE FALLS
A violent descent. There is a boat in midstream to the left of the high rock in the center.

adventurous young man who had followed life in the open since his boyhood days—a typical product of the West. Our younger brother, Ernest, who had been looking after our business in the studio at the head of the trail, was also anxious to accompany us, and we agreed to take him as far as the Bass Trail, 25 miles below.

We soon saw that we were "tenderfeet" when compared with Lauzon. Instead of walking around such rapids as he could, while we ran the boat, he would lie down on the deck (see page 76), hanging on to the bulkhead like grim death as the great waves rolled over him. Then he would shake the ice-cold water from his clothes, and, with a grin, would remark, "Young fellows, wasn't that great!" Accustomed as we were by this time to the rapids, we failed to see any great amount of pleasure in having a ton of ice-cold water dumped down the back of our necks.

Our first camp was in a grewsome spot. Just above us, several years before, we had helped cover up the skeleton of a human being (see page 75). It was found midway between the river and the plateau, lying in a natural position. The man was dressed like a prospector, and wore hob-nailed shoes, while an overcoat was buttoned around him. His pockets

A DIFFICULT RUN IN TAPEAT'S CREEK RAPID

contained Los Angeles newspapers dated May, 1900. There was nothing about him by which he could be identified. He may have been on the river and lost his boat, and starved. There was no indication that he had met a violent death.

POOR CHRISTMAS PROSPECTS

It looked for a while, on Christmas Eve, that we would have a similar fate. Ernest had left us a few hours before (see pages 82 and 83), taking out our exposed plates via Bass Trail. A rapid was reached that looked bad, still

we thought we could find a passage through. We had taken chances in rapids that looked worse, and came through unharmed; if we could run it, it would be over in a few minutes and forgotten an hour later.

Lauzon had gone as near the lower end of the rapid as he could, taking the left side, for a sheer wall of 60 feet rose from the water on the right. Ellsworth went first, taking a channel on the left. I had picked out another course on the right as being the least dangerous, but had no more than started when I found myself on a nest of rocks unable to move my boat. Other rocks were below, and the waves thundered about me.

TAKING A SHOWER BATH: OVERHANGING WALLS IN THE HAVASU CANYON SECTION

About that time I saw my brother's boat caught sideways in a reverse whirl—as they are called by rivermen—water pouring over a rock and shooting underneath, while a 2 or 3-foot wave comes up the stream and is taken down also. The *Defiance* was held between the opposing forces—the one water pouring over the rocks, the other a wave equally as high on the lower side. Finally she filled with the splashing water, sank low, and the water pouring from above caught the 1,200-pound boat and turned her over as if she were a chip. For a moment she was held; then was thrown upright and forced out by the torrent. Ellsworth had disappeared, but suddenly shot up nearly a hundred feet below, only to be carried down again with every cresting wave. If he were to be saved it must be done instantly.

I knew he would take the same chance for me, so I pried the *Edith* loose with an oar and pulled with all my might, hoping to shoot past the rocks. I was almost clear when I went over a dip, bow first, and struck another rock I had not seen. There was a thud and cracking like the

AFTER THE ACCIDENT ON CHRISTMAS EVE

The *Defiance* was overturned in a rapid above. Ellsworth Kolb, so weak from the battle in the ice-cold rapid that he could no longer swim, but kept afloat by life-preservers, was carried close to this point and crawled out, 20 feet above another rapid. Lauzon swam out from the opposite shore and saved the boat. The *Edith* was smashed while trying to follow the *Defiance*. Emery Kolb climbed the cliff on the left, but failed to see his brother, and thought he had drowned. Lauzon signaled him back as he was returning to his smashed boat. Rocks here are covered with a thin coating of ice (see text, page 83).

TYPE OF VIOLENT RAPID IN THE GRANITE GORGE

A boat can be seen in this rapid close to the wall and making pretty rough weather of it. Our camp-fires often depended on a few pieces of driftwood lodged in the rocks, as seen to the right of the picture. In the narrow sections the floods sometimes rise over 100 feet above the low-water mark.

breaking of a shingle. It was all over in a minute.

THE EDITH WRECKED

The *Edith* was a wreck; my brother had disappeared. Lauzon was climbing frantically over some boulders trying to get farther down the stream to the head of the next rapid. I could not proceed with my wrecked boat, and landed on the right in an eddy in the middle of the rapid. Climbing to the top of the rock, I looked over the next rapid, but Ellsworth was nowhere to be seen, and I had no idea that he had escaped.

I was returning to my wrecked boat when Bert called, and pointed to the foot of the cliff. Going back once more, I saw my brother in a little opening at the foot of the wall where he had climbed out, 20 feet above the next rapid. Returning to the wrecked boat, I was soon beside him.

His outer garments by this time were frozen. I soon procured blankets from my bed, removed his clothes, and wrapped him up.

Lauzon, true to our expectations of what he would do when the test came, swam out and rescued the *Defiance* before she was carried over the next rapid. Seeing that he could not aid either of us, he had bailed out. Coming across with a big grin on his face, he remarked, "Young fellows, business is picking up;" then added, "and we're losing lots of good pictures."

These experiences were our Christmas presents that year, and they were not done up in small packages, either.

QUICK REPAIRS

We repaired the wrecked boat Christmas day. Three smashed ribs on the side were replaced with mesquite which we found growing on the walls. We patched the hole with the loose bottom laid inside the boats, then painted them. A piece of canvas was tacked over this, and painted also. A piece of tin finished the repair, and the *Edith* was as seaworthy as ever.

Some of our provisions were lost or spoiled in the upset. Both sacks of flour were wet, on the outside at least. At each camp the wet sacks were placed by the fire until this wet flour hardened, and we went on using from the center as if nothing had ever happened. We caught a few fish. We felt pretty good one morning when we saw fresh meat in sight in the form of a big mountain sheep. My brother reached for his camera at the same instant that I grabbed my six shooter, but the trigger was rusted and we had no mutton stew that day.

The motion-picture camera had been under the water in our difficulties in the rapids and needed a thorough cleaning, so we held up one day and repaired it.

The next day we were again running rapids under walls 4,500 feet high. A day or two later we camped at the mouth of Havasu Canyon (Cataract Creek), but on quite a different stage of water than that we had seen when here before (see picture, page 85). It was 50 or 60 feet higher on the walls when we had worked our way down on that overland trip. At the next camp below here, New Year's eve, the walls of the inner gorge rose 3,000 feet above us and were almost sheer; then another wall rose beyond this, with a narrow plateau between. The loss of the boats in that section would quite likely have been fatal, as there was no chance of climbing out over such walls as those.

WIRELESS WARNINGS

In these sections, if it was not possible to go below the rapid to inspect it, the one who arrived first would climb out and, with signals of the hands or a flag, would direct the one who remained how to proceed, or if he ran the rapid without getting out, he would point out the hidden rocks, which looked so much like innocent waves from above the rapid. We were always endeavoring to make time. If the rapids were simply big water, without danger of an upset, we would wear a light rubber coat, so that the splashing water would freeze on the coat instead of on our clothes.

If the life-preservers were not constantly worn, they were always kept inflated and close at hand. We preferred this type of preserver to the cork on account of its light weight. For the same reason we had inflated mattresses with our sleeping bags. They saved carrying a lot of extra bed clothing, and could be thrown on the wet sand or rocky, uneven ground, and we could enjoy a comfortable night's rest. Even in their protecting sacks of rubber and canvas they looked very small when compared with the

THE HIGHEST SHEER WALLS IN THE GRAND CANYON

The inner gorge is about 3,000 feet deep. The upper walls tower about 4,500 feet above the river. In these narrow sections the floods sometimes rise 100 feet above the low-water mark. It was very cold while going through this section. Little or no sun reaches the bottom of these canyons in January, except where the course varies from its east to west direction. Cold winds would sweep down from the snow-covered cliffs above and we were constantly shifting about to keep warm.

AT THE MOUTH OF THE COLORADO RIVER, IN MEXICO

beds usually carried by the cattlemen and other men of the open.

We always kept a change of dry clothing and sometimes the films from the motion-picture camera in the bed, and as soon as the camp-fire was started a quick change was made, and the wet clothing was scattered on rocks or hung on lines close to the fire. They seldom dried entirely, and it was anything but pleasant to crawl into them the next morning.

When choosing a camp, the first thing to be considered was driftwood, as nothing but a

LOOKING NORTH TOWARD THE RIVER AT THE RAINBOW NATURAL BRIDGE

Note figure on top for comparative idea of size. The dimensions are: Height, 309 feet above the little stream; 270 feet inside of span; 30 feet wide at top of narrowest-point. The rock is softening and eroding rapidly, and the bridge will not last unless something is done to preserve it.

little mesquite grew in these lower canyons. A flood which had come down when we were in Lodore had carried most of the wood out with it, and it sometimes was very difficult to find all we needed. For this reason, if we found a good camp after 4 p.m., we usually took it. The second consideration was a quiet place to tie our boats. Both boats had been rubbed against rocks in one or two places until they were nearly worn through. The last thing we thought of was a place to throw our beds. A ledge in the rocks, an overhanging wall, an occasional cave, but usually a bed in the sand, shoveled out to fit our beds, were our choice of bed-rooms. They were always well ventilated.

With all our efforts to make headway, our usual day's run was about 10 miles, if we were in bad water. The Grand Canyon would come under this list, with its 1,700-foot fall in 200 miles. It was seldom that we had any sun in these deeper canyons (see page 85), as we traveled toward the west. In December and January it snowed several times, but the snow never descended quite to us, but turned to a chilling rain. This would freeze on the rocks, making it very poor footing; so we made no portages that were not absolutely necessary.

BELOW THE TOROWEEP

About 60 or 70 miles of this great sheerwall canyon, the walls began to break down, becoming lower and less precipitous. How long it lasted it would be hard to say, but the stream resumed its relentless sawing and cut down to its old level just as it had before, and mammoth blocks of the volcanic rock are scattered for miles along its course.

At one point in this section we imagined we saw smoke and hastened down, wondering if our new-found friend would be a prospector or a cattle-rustler. Instead of a camp-fire we found some warm springs falling 20 feet into the river. Beside the springs was a lava-filled rapid, so full of jagged sections of the volcanic rock from the cliffs that a portage was advisable. It was colder than usual this morning, and we were in the icy water a great deal as we lined and lifted the boat over the rocks at the edge of the rapid. We would stand this until numbed with the cold, then would go down and thaw out in the warmer water at the springs.

A WAYSIDE MEETING

A day's travel below this we did see some smoke, and on climbing the bank found a little, old prospector sitting in a dugout which he had shoveled out of the sand. The roar of the rapid prevented him from hearing us until we were directly in front of him.

He looked at our clothes, the rubber coats and life-preservers, then said in a matter-of-fact tone: "Well, you boys must have come by the river." After talking with him awhile we learned that he had once been wrecked in Lodore Canyon, and that Mr. Chew, who had taken Jimmie out, had supplied him with a horse and aided him on his way to civilization. His name, he told us, was Snyder, and he had just been across the river on a raft to do some assessment-work on a copper claim which he was sure would develop into a valuable mine.

He was cooking his noon meal when we arrived—two pieces of bacon and two biscuits—in a frying-pan, and with nothing else in sight; yet with true Western hospitality he invited us to stay for dinner. We thanked him, but declined, as he told us that we were but six miles above Diamond Creek, where by walking

22 miles, with a climb of 4,000 feet, we could reach the railway.

Below Diamond Creek we were surprised to find the granite walls even higher than they were above, and the rapids continued to get worse. We had imagined that the walls receded down, but the opposite was the case. It was in this last section that the three men left the Powell party, when within a little more than a day's journey from the end of the canyon. They were killed by the Indians the day after they climbed out on top.

THE LAST GREAT RAPID

Any one expecting to make this joy ride at any time will know by three pointed peaks, on the south side, that they are nearing the end of the canyon; also by a long quiescent stretch of water that they are nearing one of the worst rapids in the series. Major Powell graphically describes this rapid, located, as he said, "below a bold, lava-capped escarpment." Mr. Stone also warned us against it, stating "it was the last bad rapid in the canyon. Below that everything could be run."

On account of low water we were enabled to land at the lower end of the escarpment before beginning this portage. The river had an approximate fall of 40 feet and was filled with exposed and slightly submerged boulders from one end to the other. The roar of the rapid was deafening.

We took our boats over one bad group of rocks, lined them down, then lifted them over a second lot. The rocks were icy; there was only room for two to work, and we were weak and bruised with two other portages in much similar places. It was with a great sigh of relief that we slid our boats over this last rock, completed our fourteenth and last portage, and prepared to shoot down on the swift water that ended the rapid.

Other rapids remained, but we ran them all, with only a glance at them from the boats. We were pulling for the end. There were two more camps before we emerged into the flat country.

Many people, learning of our trip, think we are entitled to a certain degree of honor for having done something unusual. The trip is unusual and will hardly become a popular tour; but as for honor, all honor is justly due to the one who made the original exploration— Major J. W. Powell. He did not know what minute he would be confronted by a waterfall. We knew there were none. All we can say for our trip is that two or three men seldom attempted anything harder and got away with it. Our motion-picture films and plates were carried through 365 big rapids, a descent of nearly 6,000 feet, after having been on the river 101 days. We landed in Needles on January 18, one month from the time of our start from Bright Angel trail.

HOW SMITH GOT THROUGH

Among some letters awaiting us was the following, bearing the postmark of Hite, Utah:

Kolb Brothers.

Dear Friends: Well, I got here at last, after seventeen days in Cataract Canyon. The old boat will still stand a little quiet water but will never stand another rapid. I certainly played rings around some of those rocks in Cataract; I tried every scheme I had ever heard of and some that were never thought of before, but got here at last. I hope the movies are good.

Your friend,

Chas . Smith.

Another from Hite stated that Smith told him when he came to that last rapid he had carried all his equipment over the narrow ledge and was engaged in dropping his boat down with the chain, standing on the rock above, when he was suddenly jerked off into the river. He still retained his hold on the chain, pulled himself into the boat, and went through the entire rapid without oars and without upsetting, landing a mile and quarter below his supplies.

My brother afterward completed the trip into Mexico, to the Gulf of California, thus making for the second time a complete journey from Green River, Wyoming, to the tide-water.

We have just returned from a 600-mile overland trip to the reservations of the Hopi and Navajo Indians, taking in the cliff ruins of Marsh Pass and our often-thought-of Rainbow Natural Bridge.

Rising from our bed under that wonderful arch while the stars were yet in the sky, we made our way to the river, and saw a familiar turn in the wall past which we had rowed with scarcely a glance that morning two years before. Returning in time for a late breakfast, we spent a few hours in making some views; then, while the guides took the horses around the base of Navajo Mountain, we climbed the peak, sleeping under the shelving rock. Guided by signal fires, we rejoined our party the next day on the other side of the mountain and began our homeward journey over the sands of the Painted Desert.

Vol. XXVI, No. 2   WASHINGTON   June, 1921

THE GRAND CANYON BRIDGE

By Harriet Chalmers Adams

THE suspension bridge over the Colorado River in the Grand Canyon is practically completed. Late this summer it will be possible to ride from El Tovar, on the south rim of the stupendous chasm, to the Kaibab plateau, on the north rim.

The bridging of the Granite Gorge of the Colorado opens up a new wonderland in the Grand Canyon National Park. From the Kaibab plateau, which averages 1,000 feet above the better-known south rim of the canyon, new and amazing panoramas are presented.

Last month I rode down to the river over a trail not yet opened to tourists, messed with the bridge crew, and spent the night in the gorge. The bridge is 11 miles by trail from El Tovar and 4,700 feet below Yaki Point, on the Coconino plateau. The saddle trail, following the Bright Angel and Tonto trails to the river, and up Bright Angel Canyon to the Kaibab forest, is about 31 miles in length. Rim-to-rim travelers will spend the night in a camp near Ribbon Falls, about eight miles beyond the river.

It was a chilly morning when we started for the bridge camp. The wind surged through the pines and pinyons, and twisted the gnarled cypress trees overlooking the chasm. It is the Rim of the Eternal, to be approached with awe; but people differ.

I heard a stout woman, standing by the lookout, say to her daughter, "Oh! Clara, I'm terribly disappointed. We've come at a time of year when there's no water in the canyon!"

A tall man, with a red face, was explaining to a thin man in a plaid suit that, in contour, the canyon was exactly like the doughnuts his mother used to make.

SPRINGTIME ON THE TRAIL

Once down the trail it was springtime. Shimmering blue-jays chattered among the Douglas firs and emigrant butterflies zigzagged by. High in the cliff a canyon-wren piped up a love ditty.

The "expedition" consisted of the Chief Ranger of the Grand Canyon National Park, the wandering lady he escorted, and our two mules. The ranger, whose first love was the Yellowstone, has been many years in the park

BLASTING ROCK TO MAKE PLACE FOR THE FOUNDATION
OF THE GRAND CANYON SUSPENSION BRIDGE

The completed canyon bridge will be 420 feet along the roadway and is suspended 60 feet above the river in normal flow, but only 13 feet above the rushing torrent when it is at its greatest flood. This is the only bridge across the Colorado above Needles, California, which is 360 miles by river course to the south.

PACK-TRAIN CARRYING LUMBER DOWN TO THE BRIDGE SITE

"It has been a tremendous undertaking to move the lumber, cement, and cables down the 11 miles of steep, winding trail to the bridge site."

THE PACK-TRAIN MAKING ITS TORTUOUS WAY TOWARD THE RIVER BED

In transporting the material from the rim of the Grand Canyon to the suspension bridge camp site many difficulties were encountered. On one occasion one of the pack-horses went over the cliff, carrying two other animals with it. Only the resourcefulness and daring of one of the men saved the remainder of the train by cutting the ropes.

service and regards our national playgrounds with reverence. He is of the opinion that all those caught carving their names on rocks or trees should be lined up and shot at sunrise.

Down we dropped to the Tonto plateau, the green shelf on the canyon wall lying between the ruby-stained limestone and the gray Archean granite. Here winds a trail of romance.

ONCE THE HIGHWAY OF THE CLIFF-DWELLERS

In the shadowy past this was the highway of the Cliff-dwellers. Here, in later years, Spaniards whose names are not written on the historic page adventured. There came occasional fur trappers from lands far to the north;

the first of those great explorers who dared the descent of the river; hardy miners, whose half-hearted workings still border the Tonto trail.

We counted seven wild burros descended from pack animals abandoned by the miners. Deer were recently seen in this part of the canyon. Mountain-sheep hide on ledges high up the wall. Many other wild creatures still find refuge in this vast wilderness.

The only animals that we saw, besides the burros, were woodrats nearly as large as squirrels. These "trade rats" accumulate great mounds of rubbish. From a camp they walk off with the soap and the spoons, leaving pebbles and sticks in exchange.

The pack-train, carrying the bridge material from railroad to river, made its halfway camp at Pipe Creek. Here only a lonely black kitten greeted us. The pack-train was "on the job." It has been a tremendous undertaking to move the lumber, cement, and cables down the 11 miles of steep, winding trail to the bridge site. Many are the exciting tales told by the packers. On one trip a horse went over the cliff, carrying two others with him; but a resourceful lad cut the rope and saved the remainder of the train.

Since January these pack-trains have been steadily trudging up and down between the hidden river and the railroad on the rim.

A REHEARSAL FOR
CARRYING THE CABLES

The transportation of the 1,200-pound cables alone marks an epoch in bridge-building. The superintendent of the Grand Canyon National Park, who supervises the bridge-work, is an engineer whose varied experience ranges from setting the official height of Mount McKinley, in Alaska, to locating a Patagonian railroad. He conceived the idea of "rehearsing" the carrying down of the cables by estimating, with ropes, just the proper length of line necessary between each mule, as the train swung around the curves. The 1,200-pound cable was then loaded on to eight mules roped together with the weight evenly divided, a man walking at the head of each mule.

The sun was high in the heavens as we made the final drop down the newly cut trail in the granite wall to the bridge camp by the river. There were three sleeping tents in the camp, a dining-room tent, and a kitchen. The cook played star role. It is he who makes or breaks a camp. This particular cook put Broadway chefs to shame, in spite of the fact that everything but the water had to be packed down from above.

A 420-FOOT BRIDGE

I was fortunate in having the contractor himself explain the bridge to me.

The completed bridge will be 420 feet along the roadway, with a span of 500 feet from center to center of the bearings. The two main steel cables are placed about 10 feet apart and are anchored to the canyon walls 80 feet above the floor level, by means of sections of 80-pound railroad iron set into the rock with concrete.

Hanging galvanized steel cables, clamped to the main lines above, carry the wood floor of the bridge. A seven-foot wire meshing is strung along the sides as a protection for animals and pedestrians.

The bridge is 60 feet above the river in normal flow and 13 feet above the highest known water-mark in June floods. This is the only bridging of the Colorado above Needles, California, 360 miles to the south by river curve, as you "step it off" on the map.

SWINGING ACROSS THE COLORADO RIVER GORGE ON A WIRE CABLE
This method of crossing the canyon was employed during the work of constructing the suspension bridge.

THE FLYING-MACHINE, THE GRAND CANYON BRIDGE CREW CALLED IT
They went down by gravity and pulled up by hand on the other side.

Now for the bridge crew. Never have I seen a finer-looking lot of men—typical Americans, brawny, and bronzed, not a pound overweight. One used to be a lumber cruiser in Alaska; another has mined in southern Chile; a third was a cowboy "before they fenced in the whole bloomin' Southwest." One is an amateur astronomer, who spends his evenings with his telescope under the stars. He says you can see the stars better from the depths of a canyon. Several go in for photography. One has a gift for whistling and can imitate the bird calls. There is a good bit of poetry and adventure nailed into the Grand Canyon bridge.

Night in the Granite Gorge of the Colorado! They gave me the tool and meat tent for an abode. I recalled a game we played in childhood, "Heavy, heavy, hangs over your head!" It turned out to be the bacon. The framework of my tent was formerly the iron cage in which the infrequent traveler crossed the river by cable. Colonel Roosevelt crossed in this way on his ride up to the Kaibab forest.

A DEEP, MASTERFUL, SULLEN RIVER

When the camp slept and moonlight flooded the gorge, I slipped out of my sleeping-bag and walked to the river. The Colorado is a deep, masterful stream, sullen, unfriendly. No habitations border its canyon shores. It has a flow of 20,000 cubic feet per second, reaching a maximum of 200,000 cubic feet. By day its walls take on a strange, reddish-purple glow, but by moonlight they were softly pink. A weird rock, which they call the Temple of Zoroaster dominated the scene. Jupiter rode high in the heavens.

Across the river lay the ruins of an ancient Indian village, its broken stone walls strewn with prehistoric pottery—coils and Greek-key patterns—such as are found among the Mesa Verde cliff-dwellings. Perhaps it was never a permanent settlement, only a temporary winter refuge of some peaceful plateau tribe driven down from the heights by the warring Utes. The early chroniclers of the canyon did not mention these Indians.

Who will write the long-ago romances and tragedies enacted within this mighty gorge?

A chill wind swept down the canyon and I crept back to my tent.

Next morning, when the 10 o'clock sun looked over the cliff, we crossed the river in a canvas boat, rowing well upstream and coming back with the current to the landing beach. The boat leaked. It is difficult to swim the river because of the heavy sand and silt; but in case of an upset one would probably be tossed up on the rocks before reaching the rapids.

LITTLE BRIGHT ANGEL, THE BRIDGE MASCOT

We climbed the bed of Bright Angel Creek, which here enters the Colorado, to the clump of cottonwoods still called "the Roosevelt camp." Here we discovered the bridge mascot, Little Bright Angel, a gray burro who lives in Elysian Fields, with clear water, plenty of grass, and a care-free life. We fed him pancakes sent by the cook, his favorite dish.

There are 113 crossings of the creek on the trail up Bright Angel Canyon to the north rim, and the little burro knows every one of them. Not long ago he guided the foreman of the bridge-crew up to the plateau, showing him just where to cross the stream.

I had heard that a distinguished American from Philadelphia, an enthusiast over the Grand Canyon, was to be the first to cross the Grand Canyon bridge; but the foreman told

THE PACK-TRAIN ARRIVING AT THE BRIDGE CAMP,
ON THE BANKS OF THE COLORADO

The camp consisted of five tents. Three were used as sleeping quarters for the bridge crew, one for a dining-room, and the fifth for a kitchen.

me, somewhat confidentially, that Little Bright Angel would be the first fellow across.

"You see," he explained, "Bright Angel has stood so long on the north shore of the river hoping to get across. He can't swim over, and he doesn't like the canvas boat."

Up in the Kaibab forest—"the island forest," a great naturalist has called it—live wild animals which have developed on original lines. The Kaibab squirrel and its cousin, the Albert, with their broad feathery tails, are the only American squirrels with conspicuous ear-tufts.

The herd of deer, variously estimated at from 12,000 to 15,000, are the mule deer, with large, broad ears and rounded, whitish tails, tipped with black. Where there are deer, there are pumas, or mountain-lions. They call them cougars in this part of the country. Uncle Jim Owens, an old-timer on the north rim has hung out a sign: "Cougars killed to order." He has a record of 1,100 skins. His cabin walls are covered with them.

Other beasts of prey are the big gray timber-wolf, the coyote, and the fox. A man who lives here and explores unfrequented cliffs tells me there are antelope on the green shelf under the north rim. "Uncle Jim" has a promising buffalo herd, 64 in all. Isolated on a promontory and protected, the herd is sure to increase.

FURTHER READING

George Wuerthner, *Grand Canyon, A Visitor's Companion* (1998) describes the canyon's geological history and its diverse climatic conditions, while including full-color illustrations of plant and animal life found within the national park. Susan Lamb, Pam Frazier (Editor), *Grand Canyon: The Vault of Heaven* (1998) combines a dozen years of research, including conversations with the park staff and experts in geology, biology, and human history, with many area photographs.

How the Canyon Became Grand: A Short History (1998) was written by Steven J. Pyne, an environmental historian who has both walked and been transported by mule throughout the Grand Canyon's North and South Rim sections and has thoroughly studied the park's history. Michael F. Anderson, Pamela Frazier (Editor), *Living at the Edge* (1998) has the entire story of pioneer life at the Grand Canyon beginning with its infancy to the national park's opening, circa 1920, featuring 12 custom maps and 200 seldom-seen photographs.

INDEX

CONTRIBUTORS

General Editor FRED L. ISRAEL is an award-winning historian. He received the Scribe's Award from the American Bar Association for his work on the Chelsea House series *The Justices of the United States Supreme Court*. A specialist in American history, he was general editor for Chelsea's *1897 Sears Roebuck Catalog*. Dr. Israel has also worked in association with Arthur M. Schlesinger, jr. on many projects, including *The History of the U.S. Presidential Elections* and *The History of U.S. Political Parties*. He is senior consulting editor on the Chelsea House series *Looking into the Past: People, Places, and Customs*, which examines past traditions, customs, and cultures of various nations.

Senior Consulting Editor ARTHUR M. SCHLESINGER, JR. is the pre-eminent American historian of our time. He won the Pulitzer Prize for his book *The Age of Jackson* (1945), and again for *A Thousand Days* (1965). This chronicle of the Kennedy Administration also won a National Book Award. He has written many other books, including a multi-volume series, *The Age of Roosevelt*. Professor Schlesinger is the Albert Schweitzer Professor of the Humanities at the City University of New York, and has been involved in several other Chelsea House projects, including the *American Statesmen* series of biographies on the most prominent figures of early American history.